SPELLING
MADE SIMPLE

Revised Edition

SPELLING
MADE SIMPLE

REVISED EDITION

BY

STEPHEN V. ROSS, Ph.D.

MADE SIMPLE BOOKS
DOUBLEDAY & COMPANY, INC.
GARDEN CITY, NEW YORK

Library of Congress Cataloging in Publication Data

Ross, Stephen V.
Spelling made simple.

(Made simple books)
1. Spellers.   I. Title.   II. Series.
PE1145.2.R6   1981   428.1
AACR2

ABOUT THIS BOOK

You alone can determine whether you need this book. You alone know whether poor spelling causes you difficulty and embarrassment when you write business or personal letters, compositions or reports or memoranda. And you alone realize that your vocabulary is weak, flat, unvarying, inaccurate because you must use the "easy" word you can spell rather than the precise word you are unsure of.

If these symptoms are yours, then this work can help you, I am sure, a great deal. Carefully planned, it analyzes the causes of poor spelling and shows ways to eliminate them. It teaches you how to master the words you misspell most frequently and how to gain spelling mastery of words you have hitherto been afraid to use. Keyed exercises and answers help you to check your progress continually.

Since this is a book on spelling, I have not been able to deal in detail with some other aspects of language and usage. For these, I can refer the reader to no better sources than *English Made Simple* and *Word Mastery Made Simple*, both by Professors Arthur Waldhorn and Arthur Zeiger.

S.V.R.

Note: Since this work was first published, many years have passed, occasioning updating. The core of the book remains the same.

TABLE OF CONTENTS

CHAPTER FIVE

CHAPTER SIX

CHAPTER SEVEN

CHAPTER EIGHT

CHAPTER NINE

CHAPTER TEN

CHAPTER ELEVEN

CHAPTER TWELVE

CHAPTER THIRTEEN

SPELLING
MADE SIMPLE

REVISED EDITION

CHAPTER ONE

THE PROBLEM OF SPELLING

Everyone is capable of correct spelling. This is not to deny that study and patience may be necessary to achieve the best results, but correct spelling lies within everyone's reach. The motivation, the wish to spell correctly originates with you. This book presents the most efficient methods for the achievement of the goal you seek.

It goes without saying that correct spelling is one of the marks of the educated and effective man or woman. For this reason alone, you cannot permit yourself to misspell words. Nor can you—as many weak spellers do—rely upon inadequate compromises. These, in effect, *avoid* your problem. It is as easy, and of course infinitely more effective, to *solve* the problem. Afraid to try spelling the *effective* word, you may use the one you know how to spell and hope that it means almost the same thing. The dangers of this method are clear:

Incorrect usage:

We *proscribe* alcohol to remove shellac from paint brushes.

> **instead of**
> *prescribe*

or

Our day in the country was *idolic*.

> **instead of**
> *idyllic*

Stunted vocabulary:

The elderly drunkard *walked* across the street.

> **instead of**
> *staggered, tottered, reeled, swayed*

HOW THIS BOOK HELPS YOU TO SOLVE YOUR SPELLING PROBLEM

This book will help you to spell correctly those words you misspell most frequently. It will help you to avoid errors in usage. And it will make you feel more secure with those words you would like to use but have avoided lest you misspell them. Above all keep in mind that it is as simple to spell well as it is to spell badly.

How can these goals be reached? Study carefully the following pages: they detail the program that will speed your progress and lighten your task.

1. **The Core List.** Among thousands of examples, carefully analyzed, five hundred words or word-groups (for example: *to, too, two*) appeared as most commonly misspelled. (Thomas Clark Pollock's "Spelling Report," in *College English*, November, 1954.) These words and word-groups—arranged in a *descending* order of frequency of misspelling—make up the *core spelling list* placed at the head of each chapter after this one. Thus, at the head of Chapter Two you will find the forty words most commonly misspelled in English; in Chapter Three the forty words next in frequency of misspelling, and so on. You will learn *first* those words you misspell most frequently. Troublesome letters in each word have been printed in bold type to make learning easier (for example: belief, foreign).

You should master the spelling of each word in the core list before proceeding to a new chapter.

2. **Mastery Tests and Achievement Tests.** At the end of each chapter you will find a *mastery test* designed to gauge your competence. All of the core list words in the Mastery Test appear **in context**—in sentences, among other words. You will learn to spell troublesome words more readily when you see them **in action.** Sometimes the words on the core list and mastery test relate closely to the chapter they accompany. Many of the core list words in Chapter Six, for example, contain troublesome prefixes (**precede, proceed, disappoint**) or suffixes (**conceivable, admissible, characterize, arise**); Chapter Six discusses the use in spelling of prefixes and suffixes; Mastery Test Number 6 tests your achievement.

If your first efforts are not perfect, do not become discouraged—this is to be expected. The mastery tests will become progressively simpler—or at least they will seem so.

Halfway through the book and again at the close, you will take *achievement tests.* Their content: words selected from the core lists; their purpose: to help you measure your progress—and to stimulate you to continue till you have achieved mastery.

3. **The Chapters.** To make studying easier, the chapters have been arranged so that you learn *each basic step* before proceeding to the next. You will not have to memorize all the spelling rules at once; rather will you learn them singly or in small groups. Furthermore, you will learn how to improve your spelling by:

Using the dictionary (chapter 2)
Improving your pronunciation (chapter 3)
Syllabifying (chapter 4)
Interchanging parts of speech (chapter 5)
Mastering prefixes and suffixes (chapter 6)
Learning homonyms (chapter 12)
Employing memory tricks (chapter 13)

Finally, by *enjoying* the words you spell (chapter 7), you will begin to improve not only your spelling but also your vocabulary.

4. **Exercises and Tests.** Within each chapter you will find many exercises testing your skill in spelling words *other* than those on the core list. Usually these words will illustrate principles and rules discussed in the specific chapter. *Master these words too.* They will help to increase your spelling power and to develop your skill and confidence.

5. **Special Word Sections.** From the second chapter on, *special word sections* have been added at the end of each chapter. These consist of lists of *specialized* (and frequently misspelled) words used in diverse fields—business, science, art, psychology, and the like. Each of these words will appear in context. Master them; they will help you to write forcefully and correctly about the complex world in which we live.

6. **Appendixes.** At the back of the book you will find several cumulative lists of words you have learned while you have been studying:

Appendix A. Alphabetical spelling list of core words.
Appendix B. Alphabetical spelling list of words other than those on the core list.
Appendix C. Alphabetical spelling list of specialized words.

These lists provide convenient references to chapters and exercises where you may review the principles governing the spelling of a given word and also see the word in context.

7. **Supplements.** Finally, this book contains two supplementary sections which will be of great value to the reader. The first is on *pronunciation* and in so far as that aspect of speech is related to spelling problems its value is clear. The second is called *Building a Vocabulary* and treats various aspects of language as they bear on the problem of spelling. But since this section goes beyond the problem of spelling to

the wider horizon of the flexible and vivid use of language itself, it has been placed at the very end of the book. The varied, interesting, colorful, exact, and fluent use of language is your final goal—and it will be your crowning achievement.

HOW YOU CAN HELP TO SOLVE YOUR SPELLING PROBLEM

This book has been carefully planned to help you become a good speller. *But you must do your part.* Here is how you can help yourself:

1. Don't think of yourself as a poor speller. Many people—to escape embarrassment— even boast of their inability to spell. This can be harmful. Face the reality of your problem and begin to solve it by forming good habits. You must *work* in order to *learn.*

2. Keep a notebook. In it copy each word that you misspell; copy it neatly, carefully, using the dictionary as a doublecheck for accuracy. Drill on these words over and over until they are absolutely learned. A score of 98% in spelling is not enough—you can do better. *Your goal must be perfection.*

3. Analyze your difficulty. Does it stem from:
   a. Carelessness in writing, reading, listening, or pronunciation?
   b. Groups of similar words differently spelled?
   c. Varied sorts of "special" complexities such as failure to understand the meaning of the word in context, failure to use apostrophes correctly, and the like?

Eliminate the difficulty by studying the chapter that deals with your particular problem.

4. Avoid trying to study too many words at one time. The core lists usually contain forty words. *Study twenty at a time;* master these before you try the second half of the list. It is easier to learn smaller groups of words.

Before you begin work on the next chapter, take the spelling test which follows. It consists of words selected from the core list. Do not be discouraged if your score is not perfect. If you follow the directions outlined in this chapter, it will probably be perfect when you take the halfway test, certainly when you take the final test. But you must bring to the task that which you already possess—an earnest wish to learn, and the patience necessary to carry it through.

PRE-TEST OF WORDS FROM THE
CORE LIST

Underline the one correctly spelled word in each of the following groups.

1. loseing, losing, lossing
2. proceed, procede, proseed, prosede
3. hieght, heighth, height, hieghth
4. oppinion, opinion, opinnion, oppinnion
5. writing, writeing, writting, writteing
6. proffessor, profesor, proffesor, professor
7. therefor, therefore, therfor, therfore
8. foriegn, forein, forien, foreign
9. marraige, marridge, marriage, marrage
10. all right, alright, allright, all rite
11. heros, heroez, heroes, herroes
12. refered, referred, reffered, refferred
13. amachoor, amatoor, amatuer, amateur
14. atheist, athiest, atheast, athaest
15. ninty, ninety, ninedy, ninnety
16. advertisement, advertizment, advertisment, advertizement
17. leasure, leesure, leisure, liesure
18. labratory, laborattory, laboratory, labaratory
19. irestistible, irresistable, irresistible, iresistible
20. discription, description, descripttion, discripttion
21. efficeint, eficient, eficeint, efficient
22. rhythm, rythm, ryrhm, rhytm
23. embarass, embarrass, emberress, emmbarass
24. enviroment, environent, environment, envirronment
25. exaggerate, exagerate, exagerrate, exegarrate
26. prevalent, privelant, prevelant, prevelent

27. irrevelant, irrelevent, irrelevant, irelevant
28. ocurence, occurance, occurence, occurrence
29. accidently, accidentaly, accidentally, accidentilly
30. adolesence, adolecense, adolesense, adolescence
31. wierd, weard, weird, weiard
32. advantagous, advantageous, advanttagous, addvantageous
33. paralel, parralel, parallel, paralell
34. imediately, imeddiately, immediately, immediatly
35. beneficcial, benefficial, beneficail, beneficial
36. criticism, criticizm, critticism, critticizm
37. occassion, occasion, ocassion, ocasion
38. lonliness, lonelyness, loneliness, lonlyness
39. charcteristic, chrackteristic, characteristic, characteristick
40. beleif, beleaf, belief, bellief
41. acomodate, accomadate, acommodate, accommodate
42. dissapoint, disappoint, dissappoint, disapoint
43. grammer, gramar, grammar, gramer
44. athelete, atlete, athleet, athlete
45. intrest, interest, interrest, intirest
46. controversial, contraversial, controversail, contriversial
47. separite, seperate, separate, sepparate
48. maintainance, maintenance, maintenence, maintainence
49. arguement, argument, argument, arrgument
50. villein, villain, villian, villin

16

CHAPTER TWO

USING THE DICTIONARY

CORE LIST

accommodate	exist	really
achieve	existence	realize
achievement	existent	receive
all right	forty	receiving
belief	fourth	separate
believe	its	separation
busy	it's	their
business	lose	there
criticism	losing	they're
criticize	occasion	to
define	occur	too
definite	occurred	two
definitely	occurrence	
definition	occurring	

"I have a dictionary, but how can I find a word there when I don't know how to spell it?"

You have heard this query often—have perhaps made it yourself. Obviously, it would be easier to locate the troublesome word if you knew how to spell it. But even when you are in doubt, the task requires less work than you may think. Assume, for example, that you are uncertain about how to spell the kind of party you plan to attend tomorrow evening. Your first guess is "*supprise* party," but knowing it to be merely a guess, you consult the dictionary. You will not find any such word. Now what? *Suprise?* Dropping a *p* will not help. Now try this:

First—re-think the word. Then:

1. Pronounce it aloud—syllable by syllable.
2. Write down your guesses.

Probably they will be either *surprise* or *surprize*. Note that since the first syllable in each is *sur-*, your only problem now is the second syllable: *-prize* or *prise*. The dictionary will solve the problem readily—**surprise**.

3. Copy the correct spelling on the list you keep of doubtful words.

4. Memorize the correct spelling.

Another helpful way to find a word you cannot spell is to look for one close to it in meaning. Thus, if you cannot locate *fowl*, find *chicken*, whose definition reads: "a domestic *fowl*."

Exercise No. 1

Using the steps outlined above, determine which word in parentheses is correctly spelled.

1. (Litrature, Litterature, Literature) has always appealed to me because I enjoy learning about people.
2. Admiral Byrd explored the (Artic, Arctic, Arktic) regions near the North Pole.
3. Do you (reconize, recognize, recognise) that red-haired woman?
4. I relish (chocolate, choclate) malteds.
5. A good (athlete, athulete, athelete) keeps in trim.
6. Your argument is (irrevelent, irrevelant, irrelevant) to the central point.

(Cont. p. 20)

GUIDE WORDS ——

(slippery)

are shown in large type at the top of each page and indicate the first and last entries on that page.

slip·per·y (slip′ər·ē) *adj.* ·per·i·er, ·per·i·est 1 Having a surface so smooth that bodies slip or slide easily on it. 2 That evades one's grasp; elusive. 3 Unreliable; tricky. —**slip′per·i·ness** *n.*

slippery elm 1 A species of small elm with mucilaginous inner bark. 2 Its wood or inner bark.

slip·shod (slip′shod′) *adj.* 1 Wearing shoes or slippers down at the heels. 2 Slovenly; sloppy. 3 Performed carelessly: *slipshod* work.

SYLLABICATION ——

is indicated by syllabic dots dividing main entry words.

slip·stream (slip′strēm′) *n. Aeron.* The stream of air driven backwards by the propeller of an aircraft.

slip-up (slip′up′) *n. Informal* A mistake; error.

slit (slit) *n.* A relatively straight cut or a long, narrow opening. —*v.t.* **slit, slit·ting** 1 To make a long incision in; slash. 2 To cut lengthwise into strips. 3 To sever. [ME *slitten*] —**slit′ter** *n.*

slith·er (slith′ər) *v.i.* 1 To slide; slip, as on a loose surface. 2 To glide, as a snake. —*v.t.* 3 To cause to slither. —*n.* A sinuous, gliding movement. [<OE *slidrian*] —**slith′er·y** *adj.*

MAIN ENTRY ——

is shown in boldface type and consists of words, phrases or abbreviations, prefixes, suffixes and combining forms.

sliv·er (sliv′ər) *n.* 1 A slender piece, as of wood, cut or torn off lengthwise; a splinter. 2 Corded textile fibers drawn into a fleecy strand. —*v.t. & v.i.* To cut or be split into long thin pieces. [<ME *sliven* to cleave] —**sliv′er·er** *n.*

slob (slob) *n.* 1 Mud; mire. 2 *Slang* A careless or unclean person. [<Ir. *slab*]

PRONUNCIATION ——

is shown in parenthesis and follows the main entry in phonetic equivalent.

slob·ber (slob′ər) *v.t.* 1 To wet with liquids oozing from the mouth. 2 To shed or spill, as liquid food, in eating. —*v.i.* 3 To drivel; slaver. 4 To talk or act gushingly. —*n.* 1 Liquid spilled as from the mouth. 2 Gushing, sentimental talk. [ME *sloberen*] —**slob′ber·er** *n.* —**slob′ber·y** *adj.*

sloe (slō) *n.* 1 A small, plumlike, astringent fruit. 2 The shrub that bears it; the blackthorn. [<OE *slā*]

sloe gin A cordial with a gin base, flavored with sloes.

INFLECTED FORMS ——

are given when there is an irregularity of form, and present participle of verbs, the plural of nouns, and the comparative and superlative of adjectives and adverbs.

slog (slog) *v.t. & v.i.* **slogged, slog·ging** 1 To slug, as a pugilist. 2 To plod (one's way). —*n.* A heavy blow. [?] —**slog′ger** *n.*

slo·gan (slō′gən) *n.* 1 A catchword or motto adopted by a political party, advertiser, etc. 2 A battle or rallying cry. [<Scot. Gael. *sluagh* army + *gairm* yell]

slo·gan·eer (slō′gə·nir′) *Informal n.* One who coins or uses slogans. —*v.i.* To coin or use slogans.

USAGE ——

information is included when an integral part of definition follows a colon after the particular meaning to which it applies.

sloop (slōōp) *n.* A small sailboat with a single mast and at least one jib. [<Du. *sloep*]

slop¹ (slop) *v.* **slopped, slop·ping** *v.i.* 1 To splash or spill. 2 To walk or move through slush. —*v.t.* 3 To cause (a liquid) to spill or splash. 4 To feed (a domestic animal) with slops. —**slop over** 1 To overflow and splash. 2 *Slang* To show too much zeal, emotion, etc. —*n.* 1 Slush or watery mud. 2 An unappetizing liquid or watery food. 3 *pl.* Refuse liquid. 4 *pl.* Waste food or swill. [<ME *sloppe* mud]

HOMOGRAPH ——

is a word identical in spelling, having different meanings and origins and, sometimes, pronunciation. It is differentiated by a superior figure such as slop¹ and slop².

Sloop

slop² (slop) 1 A loose outer garment, as a smock. 2 *pl.* Articles of clothing and other merchandise sold to sailors on shipboard. [ME *sloppe*]

slug

an organization, or a place in a sequence. —*v.t.* **slot·ted, slot·ting** To cut a slot or slots in. [<OF *esclot* the hollow between the breasts]

sloth (slōth, slôth, sloth) *n.* **1** Disinclination to exertion; laziness. **2** Any of several slow-moving, arboreal mammals of South America. [<SLOW]

sloth·ful (slōth′fəl, slôth′-, sloth′-) *adj.* Inclined to or characterized by sloth. —**sloth′ful·ly** *adv.* —**sloth′ful·ness** *n.* —Syn. lazy, indolent, sluggish, shiftless.

slot machine A vending machine or gambling machine having a slot in which a coin is dropped to cause operation.

Three-toed sloth

slouch (slouch) *v.i.* **1** To have a downcast or drooping gait, look, or posture. **2** To hang or droop carelessly. —*n.* **1** A drooping movement or appearance caused by depression or carelessness. **2** An awkward or incompetent person. [?] —**slouch′y** *adj.* (**·i·er, ·i·est**) —**slouch′i·ly** *adv.* —**slouch′i·ness** *n.*

slough¹ (slou; slōō *esp. for def.* 2) *n.* **1** A place of deep mud or mire. **2** A stagnant swamp, backwater, etc. **3** A state of great despair or degradation. [<OE *slōh*] —**slough′y** *adj.*

slough² (sluf) *n.* **1** Dead tissue separated and thrown off from living tissue. **2** The skin of a serpent that has been or is about to be shed. —*v.t.* **1** To cast off; shed. **2** To discard; shed, as a habit or a growth. —*v.i.* **3** To be cast off. **4** To cast off a slough or tissue. [ME *slouh*] —**slough′y** *adj.*

Slo·vak (slō′väk, slō′vak) *n.* **1** One of a Slavic people of NW Hungary and parts of Moravia. **2** The language spoken by the Slovaks. —*adj.* Of or pertaining to the Slovaks or to their language. Also **Slo·vak′i·an.**

slov·en (sluv′ən) *n.* One who is habitually untidy, careless, or dirty. [ME *sloveyn*]

Slo·vene (slō′vēn, slō·vēn′) *n.* One of a group of s Slavs now living in NW Yugoslavia. —*adj.* Of or pertaining to the Slovenes or to their language. —**Slo·ve′ni·an** *adj., n.*

slov·en·ly (sluv′ən·lē) *adj.* **·li·er, ·li·est** Untidy and careless in appearance, work, habits, etc. —*adv.* In a slovenly manner. —**slov′en·li·ness** *n.*

slow (slō) *adj.* **1** Taking a long time to move, perform, or occur. **2** Behind the standard time: said of a timepiece. **3** Not hasty: *slow* to anger. **4** Dull in comprehending: a *slow* student. **5** Uninteresting; tedious: a *slow* drama. **6** Denoting a condition of a racetrack that retards the horses' speed. **7** Heating or burning slowly; low: a *slow* flame. **8** Not brisk; slack: Business is *slow.* —*v.t.* & *v.i.* To make or become slow or slower: often with *up* or *down.* —*adv.* In a slow manner. [<OE *slāw*] —**slow′ly** *adv.* —**slow′ness** *n.*

slow-mo·tion (slō′mō′shən) *adj.* **1** Moving or acting at less than normal speed. **2** Denoting a television or motion picture filmed at greater than standard speed so that the action appears slow in normal projection.

sludge (sluj) *n.* **1** Soft, water-soaked mud. **2** A slush of snow or broken or half-formed ice. **3** Muddy or pasty refuse, sediment, etc. [?] —**sludg′y** *adj.* (**·i·er, ·i·est**)

slue¹ (slōō) *v.* **slued, slu·ing** *v.t.* **1** To cause to swing, slide, or skid to the side. **2** To cause to twist or turn. —*v.i.* **3** To

---

DEFINITION
is the meaning. The order in which the different senses of the word are listed is based on frequency of usage.

ILLUSTRATION
to clarify the definitions.

RUN-ON ENTRY
is a word derived from other words by addition or replacement of a suffix, syllabified and stressed where needed.

ETYMOLOGY
is indicated in brackets following the definition giving the origin of the word when it came into the English language.

PART OF SPEECH
follow the pronunciation, and the labels in italics are abbreviated as follows: n. (noun), v. (verb-transitive), v.i. (verb-intransitive), adj. (adjective), adv. (adverb), prep. (preposition), conj. (conjunction), and interj. (interjection).

---

7. What an (interesting, intresting, interresting) hat Hermione is wearing.
8. I meet Abner Yokum (evry, every, everry) morning.
9. How can such devilish people say that their (marraige, marriage) was made in Heaven?
10. His (temprature, temperature) has risen considerably since he was operated on.

To help you progress more rapidly toward spelling mastery you should own one of the reputable modern abridged dictionaries. Used intelligently, the dictionary will help you to reduce the number of words you need to check. See sample pages (pp. 18, 19) from two of the best:

Webster's *New Collegiate Dictionary (NCD)*, 125,000 words, G. & C. Merriam Co.
The American College Dictionary (ACD), 132,000 words, Harper and Bros.

(Other reputable abridged dictionaries include:
Webster's New World Dictionary, World Publishing Co.
New College Standard Dictionary, Funk and Wagnalls Co.
Doubleday Dictionary: For Home, School & Office, Doubleday & Co., Inc.

Study these pages carefully. Observe that dictionaries provide considerably more than final authority on spelling. Indeed, almost every chapter in this book derives material from dictionaries. Your dictionary will help you to learn:

Accurate pronunciation
Correct syllabication
Correct use of capitals, hyphens, italics, and the like

Beyond these aids to spelling, your dictionary will help to extend the range of your vocabulary by providing:

The Meanings of Words
The History and Etymology of Words
Synonyms and Antonyms

And finally—by labeling words as *colloquial, slang, archaic, obsolete,* etc.—your dictionary will help you to distinguish good usage. (Consult your dictionary right now for any term which may be unfamiliar to you. Also see *Word Mastery Made Simple.*)

Keeping your dictionary beside you as you study does credit to your judgment. Good spellers—whether they are professional writers or secretaries—do so. As you master the principles of spelling described in the chapters ahead, you will need to rely on the dictionary *less* frequently. But now, at the beginning, use it freely to familiarize yourself with its resources.

Do the following exercises—based on the dictionary—before proceeding to the mastery test.

1. Give the correct pronunciation of the following words:

grimace	flaccid
quay	err
bade	debris
homicide	data
height	aerial

(Check your answers in the dictionary.)

2. Syllabify the following words:

cemetery	occurrence
aggravate	business
amateur	board
analyze	government
accommodate	eighth

(Check your answers in the dictionary.)

3. Which of the following words ought to be capitalized?

uncle joe	representative
geometry	smith of texas

pope pius xii   english
negro   spanish
french   democracy
     thursday

(Check your answers in the dictionary.)

4. Indicate the correct usage label after each of the following words:

petrol   hugger-mugger
sharpie   goner
corking   boom town
e'er   hangout
hotrod   billabong

(Check your answers in the dictionary.)

Mastery Test Number 1

Do not proceed to the next chapter until you have taken this test. Master the spelling of these words from the *core list* before you try to learn those in the chapters ahead. Remember: in spelling your goal is a perfect score.

I. Choose the appropriate word for each blank. Note that in some instances though all the parenthetic words are correctly spelled, only one is appropriate *in context*.

EXAMPLE: In the forest, we watched the ...... eating leaves.

(a. dear   b. deer)

Answer: b. *deer*

1. There, at the end of the rainbow— ...... a pot of gold. (a. its   b. it's   c. its')
2. Men ...... play roles in family life. (a. too   b. two   c. to)
3. You say ...... coming, but are they? (a. their   b. they're   c. there)
4. Why so much ado about so little ...... do? (a. to   b. too   c. two)
5. Look ......! The unicorn has lost its horn. (a. there   b. their   c. they're)

6. ...... ductility makes copper useful for wire. (a. It's   b. Its'   c. Its)
7. Don't ...... interest; the plot becomes more absorbing as you go on. (a. loose   b. lose)
8. St. Louis finished ...... in the National League that year. (a. fourth   b. forth)
9. ......, how can you dislike caviar? (a. Really   b. Realy   c. Reely)
10. Ruth could not bear ...... from Na-omi. (a. separation   b. seperation   c. separetion)

II. One of the core list words in each of the following sentences needs an *extra* letter to make it correct. Add the necessary letter.

EXAMPLE: Begin at the begining. *begin-ing* lacks an *n*—begin*n*ing

1. After forty days it occured to Noah that he and his shipmates had reached their destination.
2. Joe's busness is all right, but he is losing his hair anyhow.
3. Do you really believe that you can ac-comodate both customers and cousins?
4. May I take this ocasion to criticize your achievement?
5. Definitly! I really welcome criticism.

III. One of the core list words in each of the following sentences contains an *extra* letter that causes a misspelling. Remove the extra letter.

EXAMPLE: The sun is shinning brightly. shin*n*ing should be *shining*

1. Your deffinition of beauty is open to criticism on two counts.
2. In an atomic era, man's exsistence often seems to lose is significance.

3. Separate those two brawlers and ask them too leave.

4. I want you two believe that because it is true.

5. Fourty parties in two months keep any bachelor busy.

IV. One word in each of the following groups is correctly spelled. Choose the word.

EXAMPLE: I respect your (*choice*, choise, choose, choyce)

1. Aaron predicted that the revolution would (occur, ocurr, occurr) on schedule.
2. Belial fought a (loosing, loseing, losing) battle against the heavenly host.
3. Citron loved to (receave, receive, recieve) crabapples for his birthday.
4. Diomedes did not (beleive, beleave, believe) that Hector could outfight him.
5. Ezekiel kept (buzy, bussy, busy) counting bones in Desert Valley.
6. Franchot is handsome (all right, alright, allright).
7. Geoffrey's finest (achievement, acheivement, achievment) is not in mathematics.
8. Hildegarde never could (seperate, separate, saparate) men from boys.
9. Irving disliked personal (critcizm, criticism, critisism).
10. James did not (realize, realise, reallize) the absurdity of his argument.

V. Proofread (that is, correct) the following paragraph, correcting all errors in spelling.

The beleif that one can acheive perfection in spelling is well-founded. Most helpful would be a deffinite plan of study aimed at eliminating obvious errors like *receiving* for *recieving*; *occurring* and *occurrence* for *occuring* and *occurence*; and *exist* and *existance* for *exsist* and *existence*.

SPECIAL WORD SECTION—BUSINESS

Here is the first of the *special word sections*. The words listed below appear frequently in business correspondence, reports, and the like. Often they are misspelled. Master their spelling; then test your *knowledge* of their *spelling* and *meaning* in the exercises that follow.

Even if these twenty words are not those of your specialization, learn them. You can benefit by knowing how to spell and use words centrally important for understanding the complex world in which you live.

accountant	liability
acknowledgment	liquidate
auditor	management
collateral	merchandise
coupon	mortgage
dunning	negotiable
embezzle	personnel
entrepreneur	promissory
franchise	syndicate
ledger	tariff

Special Word Exercise No. 1

I. Complete the following sentences by choosing the appropriate word from the list below. *If any word in the list is incorrectly spelled, correct it.*

1. A high ...... on imported watches raises their price on the American market.
2. Recent purchases of ...... are entered on the ....
3. The ...... of the soda water company issued a ...... to two bottling companies, giving them permission to use the company's label.

frandchize managment tarrif
merchandise ledger

II.

1. The ......, when he examined the company's books, discovered that $10,000 had been ....
2. How much ...... must I offer to procure the loan?
3. After you sign this check, it will become ....
4. The ...... manager interviewed six candidates for the position of floorwalker.

> colatteral   embezzeled   personnal
> negotiable   auditer

III.

1. When Jones failed to pay his ...... note, his creditor sent him a strong ...... letter.
2. An efficient ...... makes his credit and debit ledgers balance.

3. My favorite pastime is clipping stock ...... and estimating their value.

> coupons   duning   acountant
> promisery   liabillity

IV.

1. Our ...... pooled its finances and invested in government bonds.
2. A man who underwrites the expense of a business is known as an ....
3. Although I wrote to the bank inquiring about a second ...... on my house, I have received no ...... from them.
4. To raise money to pay debts, the company was compelled to ...... its surplus stock.

> liquidate   morgage   enterprener
> acknowledgement   sindicate

CHAPTER THREE

SOUND SPELLING: THE USE OF PHONETICS

CORE LIST

affect	disastrous	surprise
among	effect	than
athlete	effective	then
athletic	environment	thorough
began	government	weather
begin	governor	whether
beginning	interest	woman
benefit	interpret	women
beneficial	interpretation	write
benefited	marriage	writer
choose	personal	writing
chose	personnel	written
choice	shining	
condemn	similar	

For more than two hundred years, earnest and scholarly men have tried—with limited success—to establish a logical relationship between the sound (**phonetics**) and the spelling of English words. During the mid-eighteenth century Benjamin Franklin—a fine printer among other things—recognized and tried to correct phonetic inconsistencies that permitted a man to write a "*messeg* to his *yf*" (instead of *message, wife*). But despite Franklin's efforts and those of countless others, George Bernard Shaw, writing his *Preface to Pygmalion* in 1900, observed with some justification: "No man can teach himself what English should sound like from reading it."

In some languages, words are spelled as they sound—each letter has its fixed correspondent in sound. Because in English the twenty-six letters of our alphabet provide no such correspondence, certain difficulties arise to plague both speaker and speller:

I. Pronunciation may change while spelling remains the same

Vowels ea	At work he takes the lead He does not fear cold lead Nor is he moved to tears When he his clothing tears.

NOTE: A vowel is an uninterrupted speech sound—*a, e, i, o, u,* sometimes *w* and *y*—made through the middle of the mouth.

Consonants ough	Though the **tough cough** and **hiccough plough** me **through**. O'er life's dark **lough** my way I still pursue.

NOTE: A consonant is a speech sound made with some interruption of the breath stream. Furthermore, consonants do not have so strong a *sound* quality as vowels. For example, *i* in *hit* has a stronger sound than either of the consonants, *h* or *t*.

II. Spelling may change while pronunciation remains the same

Vowels	a. moon, do, cruise, rendez-vous, Hindu, ragout, sue.

oo b. good, look, roof.
    c. door, floor.
    d. zoology.

Consonants a. **q**uery, **q**ueen, **c**ousin, **k**ite, **kh**an.

k and c b. tal**k**, li**k**e, anti**q**ue, li**qu**or.
    c. ex**c**ept, hibis**c**us, bis**c**uit.
    d. a**cc**ount, a**cq**uaint.

III. Both spelling and pronunciation may change

Thus, Old English *skip* has become modern *ship;* yet Old English *skipper* remains unchanged.

At this point, like Koko in *The Mikado*, perhaps you feel ready to say, "Here's a state of things; here's a pretty mess." But do not despair. At worst you may conclude that with certain sounds in English, no rules are effective. In such cases you have no choice but to learn the word. However, what is far more important is that you can improve your spelling by carefully attending to your pronunciation. As you learn the principles of effective pronunciation, you should be able to master that sizeable group of words (many of which appear on the core list for this chapter) commonly misspelled because they are commonly mispronounced.

Here is the cardinal rule in "sound" spelling:

Say the word slowly *before* you spell it, *as* you spell it, and again *after* you have spelled it.

You will find it helpful also to *break the word into syllables*. Carefully pronounce each syllable; write the word as you say it, and then pronounce it again.

Keep these principles in mind as you study the groups of "sound" problems below.

"LOST" VOWELS

Do not "lose" vowels. *Find* them in the list below by pronouncing the boldfaced *vowel* carefully:

cruel
Pronounce e as in over   **not** cr**oo**l

boundary
Pronounce a as in alone   **not** bound**r**y

chocolate
Pronounce o as in company **not** choc**l**ate

every
Pronounce e as in over   **not** ev**r**y

poem
Pronounce e as in hen   **not** p**o**me

ruin
Pronounce i as in inn   **not** r**u**ne

interested
Pronounce e as in over   **not** int**r**ested

superintendent
Pronounce e as in over   **not** sup**r**intendent

sophomore
Pronounce o as in company **not** sop**h**more

Niagara
Pronounce a as in alone   **not** Niag**r**a

Exercise No. 2

Choose the correctly spelled word. Watch for "lost" vowels. Pronounce each word within the parentheses before you make your choice.

1. Stop picking those (a. vilets, b. vielets, c. violets).
2. Where do you keep your (a. jewels, b. jewls, c. jools)?
3. Oscar knocked my hat off (a. accidently, b. accidentally, c. accidentaly).
4. Edgar's (a. temperament, b. temprament, c. temparament) is always genial.
5. (a. Incidently, b. Incidentally, c. Incidentaly), I will not be able to meet you for supper.

6. Election to an honor society is a (a. priviledge, b. privlege, c. privilege) few students can hope for.
7. Most adolescent girls tell their deepest secrets to a (a. diry, b. dairy, c. diary).
8. Little boys get less pleasure from (a. minature, b. miniture, c. miniature) trains than do their fathers.
9. Strephon has been elected to (a. parliment, b. parlament, c. parliament).
10. Henry does his best, but his grades in (a. mathematics, b. mathmatics, c. mathamatics) are poor.

"LOST" CONSONANTS

Do not "lose" consonants. *Find* them in the list below by pronouncing the boldfaced *consonant* carefully:

Arctic (pronounced Arktic)
government
candidate
probably
February
library
length (pronounced lenkth)
told

Exercise No. 3

Choose the correctly spelled word. Watch for "lost" consonants. Pronounce each word within the parentheses before you make your choice.

1. We regard the Joneses as (a. acquaintances, b. aquaintances, c. akwaintances), not as intimate friends.
2. Junior always replies, (a. "Alright," b. "Allright," c. "All right,") when his mother calls.
3. I lack the (a. strnth, b. strenkth, c. strength) to lift the heavy bar bells.
4. What election (a. district, b. districk, c. distric) do you vote from?

5. Ingres sketched in the (a. backround, b. background, c. baground) before he added figures.
6. Do as I (a. tole, b. tol, c. told) you.
7. We argue (a. stricly, b. strickly, c. strictly) according to logic.
8. I agree, but my (a. partner, b. pardner, c. partoner) may not.
9. Your meager objections to his proposal seem (a. irrevelent, b. irrelevant, c. irrelevent).
10. He insists that his cast perform (a. egsactly, b. exsactly, c. exactly) as he directs.

SILENT PARTNERS

Because vowels sometimes lose their identity in unaccented syllables, you may become confused about the spelling of a word you hear pronounced quite correctly. For example, listening to someone pronounce **relative** (the accented syllable is **rel**, the unaccented **ative**) fails to help you to determine whether to spell it *relitive, reletive,* or correctly—relative. That weak vowel (**a**) in the unaccented syllable—the silent partner—causes the trouble.

You can help yourself to solve the problem posed by weak vowels by thinking of another word in the same family. Thus, think of relate and you should not misspell **relative**; think of humor and you should not misspell **humorous**; think of victor and you should not misspell **victorious**.

Exercise No. 4

Provide the missing vowel for each word in the following pairs:

1. acad.my   acad.mic
2. compet.tive   compet.tion
3. m.stery   m.sterious
4. r.dicule   r.diculous
5. ap.logy   ap.logetic
6. friv.lous   friv.lity
7. coll.ge   coll.giate

8. ben.fit   ben.ficial
9. pol.tics   pol.tical
10. med.cine   med.cinal
11. hypocr.sy   hypocr.tical, hypocr.te
12. d.spair   d.sperate
13. defin.te   defin.tion, defin.tive
14. temp.rate   temp.rature
15. gramm.r   gramm.tical

Like weak vowels, consonants—in certain combinations—also lose their sound value. When the consonants occur in combinations at the beginning of a word, the first letter usually (though not always) remains silent:

gnarled   pronounce it **narled**—the g is silent
gnaw   naw
gnat   nat

(Note, however, ghost, where the first letter is sounded—**gost**.)

Knowledge, knife, knew, knight, knot are a few among more than forty words beginning with **kn**, in all of which the k is silent.

In pneumonia, pneumatic, psychic, psychology, psalm, and the like, the p is silent.

In write, wring, wrought, wreck, wreath, and the like, the w is silent.

Sometimes, however, the **second** letter is the silent partner as in sword or scythe:

rhyme   pronounce it **rime**—the h is silent
rhythm   **rithum** (th as in the)
rheumatism   roomatism
rhetoric   retorik
rhapsody   rapsody

Silent consonants sometimes appear in the middle of a word: calm, debt, doubt, diaphragm, night, often; or at the end of a word: autumn, column, condemn, hymn, though, and through. With such words you should study the troublesome consonants carefully and memorize the correct spelling.

UNWANTED AND CONFUSED GUESTS

Another trouble spot in pronunciation and consequently in spelling is the sound that appears where it does not belong—the unwanted guest who spoils the party and the spelling. Attend carefully to the pronunciation of the following words. Note how letters erroneously intrude and distort the correct sound—and, as a result, possibly cause spelling errors.

Say and Write	
across	**not** acros*t*
once	**not** onc*t*
attack	**not** attack*t*
attacked	**not** attack*t*
mischievous	**not** mischie*v*ious
grievous	**not** grie*v*ious
film	**not** fil*u*m
athletic	**not** ath*e*letic
height	**not** heigh*th*
column	**not** col*y*umn
drowned	**not** drow*n*ded
escape	**not** ex*c*ape

When you rid yourself of these "unwanted guests," try not to confuse those who remain. Keep your sounds in order; **avoid interchanging sounds** in speech or in spelling:

Say and Write	
children	**not** child*ern*
irrelevant	**not** irre*vel*ant
hundred	**not** hund*erd*
modern	**not** mod*ren*
perspiration	**not** *pres*piration
larynx	**not** lar*nyx*
bronchial	**not** bron*ich*al

Mastery Test Number 2

Do not proceed to the next chapter until you have taken this test. Master the spelling of these words from the core list before you try to learn those in the chapters ahead. Remember: in spelling your goal is a perfect score.

I. In each of the italicized words in the following sentences, a blank space has been left for *one* letter. If a letter should be added to make the spelling correct, add it. If the word is correct as is, ignore the blank space and leave the word as is.

EXAMPLE: Liquor has *ru.ned* many men.

Add an *i* to spell *ruin*
We are *din.ing* out.
Dining is correct. Add nothing

1. Vera has *writ.en* her autobiography.
2. Ulysses won many *ath.letic* events.
3. Thomas arrived early for Winnie's *su.prise* party.
4. Stephen took little *int.rest* in girls until he was five years old.
5. Randy has a *shin.ing* light in her eyes since Clem proposed.
6. Quincy inherited his father's interest in affairs of *gover.ment*.
7. Percy's *enviro.ment* encouraged him to develop artistic tastes.
8. Oliver owned a yacht *simil.ar* to Percival's.
9. Newton searched for an apple *amo.ng* his miscellaneous notebooks.
10. Melissa is *begin.ing* to resemble her father, but she may outgrow it.

II. Choose the appropriate word for each blank. Note that in some instances though all the parenthetic words are correctly spelled, only one is appropriate in context.

1. We shall attend the lawn party ...... the ...... is pleasant or not. (weather, whether, wether)
2. When he offered me two alternatives, I ...... the second of them. Which would you ......? (chose, choosed, choose) Why is your choice more ......? (affective, effective, efective)
3. What may ...... you need have no ...... *upon me*. (affect, afect, effect)
4. I have a ...... interest in the man the ...... director is considering for that new job. (personnal, personnel, personal)
5. Oh men, oh ...... (wimmin, woman, women)

III. One word in each of the following groups is correctly spelled. Choose the word.

1. The (governnor, governer, governor) of the state put in (writting, writing, writeing) his approval of the new industrial plant.
2. What (interpretation, interpertation, interpitation) of the law compels you to (condem, condenm, condemn) an innocent man?
3. (Marraige, Marriage, Marridge) proves (benificial, beneficial, benefical) to some, (disastrous, disasterous, disastarous) to others.
4. Before I vote for the new expressway, I should like to make a (through, thorough, thoro) investigation of the expenditures involved.
5. What possible (benifit, benefit, bennefit) will you gain from quitting your job?

IV. Proofread the following paragraph, correcting all errors in spelling.

Then the athelete began to write. He knew that during this examination he would have to begin to interpet his material because his chooice of one strand of evidence rather then another would reveal whether he had benefitted from his teacher's efforts to show him how to think and writte.

SPECIAL WORD SECTION—LAW

The words listed below appear frequently in legal correspondence, contracts, and the like. Often they are misspelled. Master their spelling; then test your knowledge of their *spelling* and *meaning* in the exercises that follow.

abandonment	bigamy
accessory	burglary
adjudicate	coercion
affidavit	counsellor-at-law
alibi	defendant
alimony	homicide
annul	indictment
arraign	subpoena
bailiff	usury
bankrupt	writ

Special Word Exercise No. 2

Complete the following sentences by choosing the appropriate word from the list below. *If any word in the list is incorrectly spelled, correct it.*

I.

1. Because he was accused of . . . . . ., the defendant agreed to . . . . . . all but one of his several marriages.
2. When a husband deserts his wife, the law terms his act . . . . . ., and his wife may sue for . . . .
3. Having helped the thief to escape, his sister was arrested as an . . . . . . after the fact.

> accessary bigimy annull
> allimoney abandonment

II.

1. The accused . . . . . . had a plausible . . . .

2. The state prosecutor sought to obtain an . . . . . . against the man charged with . . . .
3. Policemen are not permitted to use . . . . . . to force a confession from a prisoner.

> alibbi burglery inditement
> coercion defendent

III.

1. Lacking funds or property with which to pay his debts, the . . . . . . filed an . . . . . . notifying his creditors of his situation.
2. The judge issued a . . . . . ., a court order which the . . . . . . found harmful to his client's rights.
3. The witness received a . . . . . . ordering him to testify in court.

> afidavitt bankrup writt
> subpoena councilor-at-law

IV.

1. The disputants asked the judge to . . . . . . their differences.
2. The . . . . . . escorted the accused murderer to the judge's bench, where the judge began to . . . . . . the prisoner on charges of . . . .
3. One who charges illegal interest rates for loans is guilty of . . . .

> ajudicate araign baillif
> homicide usury

CHAPTER FOUR

THE HYPHEN: DIVIDER AND COMBINER

CORE LIST

acquaint	immediate	privilege
acquaintance	immediately	probably
category	incident	professor
comparative	incidentally	profession
conscience	intelligent	psychology
conscientious	loneliness	recommend
conscious	lonely	repetition
controversy	necessary	succeed
controversial	noticeable	success
describe	perform	useful
description	performance	useless
exaggerate	possess	using
experience	possession	
explanation	prejudice	

The hyphen [a short line (-)]* may be used *to divide* words or *to combine* them. Because exceptions modify a considerable number of the "rules" affecting the use of hyphens, only those rules generally applicable have been included here. When you are uncertain your dictionary will resolve your doubts.

DIVIDER

As a divider the hyphen is used chiefly to break a word into syllables—especially at the end of a line. For the sake of neatness and of clarity you should try, wherever possible, to avoid such division. Occasionally, however,

---

* Distinguish between the hyphen (a short line) and the dash (a long mark used only in punctuation).

---

you may find it advantageous to syllabify rather than to leave one line obviously shorter than those preceding or following. Thus, the following rules will help you to divide and conquer your problems of syllabication. You will find such knowledge especially useful for neat and accurate typing.

Divide syllables according to pronunciation:

quar-tet	mid-get	pro-ceed
tire-some	hack-ney	pat-ent
mid-dle	ab-surd	
pro-mote	our-selves	

When words exceed two syllables, continue where possible to divide according to pronunciation, but strive to maintain a meaningful syllable. For example, **depart-ment** is better than department; **hyper-bole** is better than hy-per-bole; **sarsa-parilla** is better than *sar-sa-pa-ril-la*. Try your skill at dividing the following: **dramatization, happiness, harbinger, inextricable, persecute, perpendicular, pretentious, responsible, sophistication, tonsillectomy.** Use your dictionary to check your results.

When two consonants stand together between two vowels, divide between the consonants. For example, in the word **tipple**, the vowels i and e encompass the consonants pp; consequently, the syllabic division occurs between the consonants—**tip-ple.** Apply this principle to the following words: **passion, sarcasm, mountain, million, Indian, running, structure, important, pasture, tripping.**

Avoid these pitfalls in syllabication:

1. Never divide one-syllable words.

Write **wrong**   not *wr-ong*
 right   not *ri-ght*
 which   not *wh-ich*
 breadth   not *bre-adth*
 spared   not *spar-ed*

2. Never divide a word after a single letter.

Write **abroad**   not *a-broad*
 enough   not *e-nough*
 alone   not *a-lone*
 among   not *a-mong*
 unite   not *u-nite*

3. Never devide on a syllable with a silent vowel.

Write **passed**   not *pass-ed*
 pained   not *pain-ed*
 people   not *peo-ple*
 helped   not *help-ed*
 spelled   not *spell-ed*
 paired   not *pair-ed*

4. Wherever possible, avoid divisions that demand two-letter syllables.

Write **until**   not *un-til*
 only   not *on-ly*
 stricken   not *strick-en*
 money   not *mon-ey*
 heaven   not *heav-en*

Exercise No. 5

Syllabify among the following words only those able to be divided if they appear at the end of a line:

buoyant climbed even changing country losses onus
criticism amen noisy unite running often passage
dwindling idol vexed sizzling about excessive

COMBINER

As a combiner the hyphen fuses parts into a new whole, expresses a unit idea. When words first become associated, they are generally written separately. Later the hyphen—a half-way mark—is used to join them. When the combination becomes thoroughly familiar, the tendency is to omit the hyphen and to write the word as a solid unit:

First Stage		Second Stage	Third Stage
basket	ball	basket-ball	basketball
class	room	class-room	classroom
down	town	down-town	downtown
up	town	up-town	uptown
proof	reader	proof-reader	proofreader
book	keeper	book-keeper	bookkeeper
dress	maker	dress-maker	dressmaker
tax	payer	tax-payer	taxpayer
school	boy	school-boy	schoolboy
working	man	working-man	workingman

Because the hyphen is a transitional mark, however, its use varies. Authorities disagree about which compounds ought to be written solid, which separate, and which hyphenated. The suggestions given below will apply to a majority of circumstances, but the best principle seems to be: When in doubt consult the current edition of a good dictionary.

Hyphenate:

1. Two or more words used as a single adjective and preceding their noun.

first-rate man
iron-clad contract
out-of-date idea
salt-water fishing
much-needed vacation
better-trained worker
well-known writer
never-to-be-forgotten experience
most-favored-nation clause

2. Two or more words used as a single part of speech.

ne'er-do-well	go-between
hero-worship	forget-me-nots
dog-tired	goof-off
life-history	quiet-spoken
cross-reference	editor-in-chief

3. Two or more words when the last is a participle.

foul-*smelling* garbage	stem-*wound* watch
ready-*made* suit	L-*shaped* living room
interest-*bearing* note	war-*torn* nations
fun-*loving* boy	worm-*eaten* apple
hard-*working* girl	foreign-*born* citizen

4. Compounds in which the first element is *self* or *ex* (meaning "former").

self-satisfied	self-reliance	self-made
ex-champion	ex-G.I.	ex-student
self-assured	self-hate	
ex-president	ex-wife	

5. Compound numbers, compound fractions, and fractions used as adjectives.

twenty-one years—compound number
twenty-one twenty-fifths—compound fraction
two-thirds majority—fraction used as adjective

6. Words that would otherwise bring together:

a. Three identical consonants
   ha*ll-l*amp   gra*ss-s*eed   she*ll-l*ike
b. Two identical vowels
   co-author pre-eminent re-echo pro-ally
   co-operate (Note: Also written *cooperate*)
c. A lower-case letter and a capital letter
   un-American   pre-Christian
   anti-Semitism   U-boat   pro-British

Exercise No. 6

Place the hyphen between the words requiring hyphenation.

a. His anti vivisectionism alienated the single minded fanatics.
b. The mop up over, the victorious leader of the opposition pledged that his government would adopt a pro United States middle road government.
c. Connecticut will turn darkness into daylight on the most heavily traveled section of its new turnpike in the hope of cutting night time accidents.
d. An all night session left the legislators weary, knee deep in unfinished business, and still lacking the two thirds majority to defeat the bill against filibustering.
e. All cargo transport planes offer dependable on time deliveries to eighty-six countries and territories on all six continents. By lighter packing, lower insurance rates, less transshipment, they compete with other shipping media.

Mastery Test Number 3

Do not proceed to the next chapter until you have taken this test. Master the spelling of these words from the **core list** before you try to learn those in the chapters ahead. Remember: in spelling your goal is a perfect score.

I. One of the core words in each of the following sentences needs an *extra* letter to make it correct. Add the necessary letter.

EXAMPLE: Begin at the begining.
Begi*n*ing should be beginning.

1. Advertisers who exagerate the worth of their products deserve to be punished.
2. Immediatly after the party Luella returned to her garret.
3. I should like, incidentaly, to add one more point to my argument.
4. His head is scarcely noticable between his ears.
5. Rank has its privlege, but I have no rank.
6. A toy gun was found in the posession of the youthful burglar.
7. May I aquaint you with the facts of life?
8. I am barely concious of any events going on about me.
9. To escape lonliness many people seek the company of other lonely souls.
10. Is it necesary always to shout in my presence?

II. One word in each of the following groups is correctly spelled. Choose the word.

1. Leonard has no (predjudice, prejudice, perjudice) towards foreigners.
2. Maximilian has an (inteligent, intelligent, intelligant) approach to financial problems—he neither lends nor borrows.
3. Nestor loved to recall his (experience, expereince, experiance) as a warrior.
4. Oliphant was a (conscientous, conscientious, consientious) worker who gave more to his job than was called for.

5. Franz Ferdinand's morganatic marriage became a (contreverisal, contraversial, controversial) issue upon which many opinions were voiced.
6. Queequeg developed more than a casual (acquaintance, accqaintance, acquaintence) with Ishmael.
7. Raskolnikov's (performance, performence, perrformance) with an axe left little to be desired.
8. Sylvia gave a vivid (discription, descripion, description) of the murderer's apparel.
9. Timothy may have been a (comparitive, comparative, compparitive) newcomer, but his talents were undeniable.
10. Uriah heaped lavish attention upon his parakeet, but could never get it to (preform, perform, perrform).

III. In each of the italicized words in the following sentences, a blank space has been left for one letter. Add the appropriate letter.

1. How would you *d.scribe* your *profes-.ion?*
2. His refusal to answer will *prob.bly* start a *contr.versy.*
3. The latest border *inc.dent* between these nations is merely a *rep.ttion* of what has passed between them many times before.
4. If you choose the *cat.gory* of eating, you will certainly *suc.eed* in answering all questions.
5. Have you tried *us.ng psyc.ology* to influence your children?

IV. Proofread the following paragraph, correcting all errors in spelling.

The lonly proffessor tried without sucess to search his conscience for an explaination of his feeling that he was usless. But no imediate answer was forthcoming. No useful guide led him to truth; no friend could reccomend a potion that might posess special powers to help him.

SPECIAL WORD SECTION—BIOLOGY

The words listed below appear frequently in popular articles about biology as well as in books. Master their spelling; then test your knowledge of their *spelling* and *meaning* in the exercises that follow.

amphibian	fungus
anatomy	heredity
bacilli	instinct
botany	mammal
carbohydrate	microscope
carnivorous	organism
chlorophyll	parasite
chromosome	protoplasm
embryo	vertebrate
evolution	zoology

Special Word Exercise No. 3

Complete the following sentences by choosing the appropriate word from the list below. *If any word in the list is incorrectly spelled, correct it.*

I.

1. Turtles, because they live on either land or sea, are known as . . . .
2. In the science of . . . . . ., one may encounter the . . . . . . of an ape, whereas in . . . . . ., one is more likely to examine . . . . . . and other forms of plant life.
   zology, amphibbian, fungus, embrio, bottany

II.

1. The wolf, a . . . . . . animal, prefers chickens for his diet rather than daisies.
2. Whales have backbones and milk glands. Like us they are . . . . . . and . . . .
3. In the . . . . . . of life from its primitive stages, all forms of nature have been afflicted with . . . .

   mammel, carniverous, vertebrate, parisite, evilution

III.

1. By looking into a powerful . . . . . ., you can study a living . . . . . . too small to be seen with the naked eye.
2. Certain parts of our . . . . . ., such as our facial characteristics, height, and the like, are the result of our . . . .
3. Responses which we cannot control—hunger, fear, thirst—we attribute to . . . .

   heredety, instinkt, anattomy, microscope, organizm

IV.

1. . . . . . . may color your plants green, but it cannot make goats smell sweet.
2. Bacteria that cause disease are known as . . . . . .
3. Unless a plant contains . . . . . ., the essential matter of all life, it cannot produce the starchy substance known as . . . .
4. Each . . . . . . contains genes, the elements that determine our hereditary traits.

   bacili, carbohydrate, clorophil, chromocom, protoplasim

CHAPTER FIVE

SPELLING BY PART OF SPEECH: NOUN AND VERB

CORE LIST

advice	grammar	prevalent
advise	hero	principal
analyze	heroes	principle
analysis	heroine	prominent
apparent	heroic	pursue
appear	height	rhythm
appearance	imagine	sense
approach	imaginary	studying
approaches	imagination	tried
consistent	led	tries
consistency	Negro	varies
embarrass	Negroes	various
foreign	passed	
foreigners	past	

Nouns and verbs structure each sentence you write or speak. When they are concrete and vivid these parts of speech clarify and invigorate what you wish to communicate. Misspelling destroys the effect you labor to achieve. This chapter teaches you how to identify the troublespots in spelling nouns and verbs and how to eliminate them.

THE PARTS OF SPEECH

PART OF SPEECH. The term **part of speech** refers to the job that a word does in a sentence—to its **function or use.** Since there are eight separate jobs, words are divided into eight classes or **eight parts of speech:** noun, pronoun, verb, adjective, adverb, preposition, conjunction, interjection.

JOB, FUNC-TION, USE	PART OF SPEECH	EXAMPLES
1. To name a person, place, thing, quality, state, or action.	Noun	Adam, Washington, pen, wit, joy, laughter.
2. To substitute for a noun.	Pronoun	he, she, it.
3. To express action—or non-action (state of being).	Verb	run, talk, think. is, was, will be.
4. To modify (describe or limit) the noun and pronoun.	Adjective	*strong* man, *ugly* city, *limited* quantity, *few* hours.
5. To modify any verb, adjective, or adverb.	Adverb	think *quickly*, *unusually* ugly, *very* quickly.
6. To show the relationship between a noun or pronoun and some other word.	Preposition	cart *before* horse, dog *in* manger, bombs *over* Brooklyn.
7. To join two words or two groups of words.	Conjunction	Jack *and* Jill; candy is dandy *but* liquor is quicker.
8. To display emotion.	Interjection	Oh! Gosh! Heigh-ho! Hurrah!

A word is a noun, verb, adjective, or other part of speech, depending on its use—and on

its use only. That is to say, a word is a noun if it is used like a noun, if it names; it is a preposition if it is used like a preposition, if it shows the relationship between nouns; and so on. In the following passage note that the word **round** is used in **five** different ways:

Our *round* world—which I shall *round* once more before I die—spins *round* and *round* on its axis, at the same time making a circle *round* the sun that results in the *round* of the seasons.

a. *round* world—adjective, because it modifies the noun *world*.

b. I shall *round*—verb, expresses action.

c. spins *round* and *round*—adverb, modifies verb *spins*.

d. circle *round* the sun—preposition, shows relationship between two nouns, *circle* and *sun*.

e. *round* of the reasons—noun, names something.

Exercise: (This exercise is worked out as a model)

Indicate the part of speech of the italicized words:

> *Jack and Jill went up* the *hill*
> To fetch a *pail of water.*
> *Jack fell down* and *broke his crown*
> *And Jill came* tumbling *after.*

Word	Part of Speech	Reason
Jack	noun	names a person
and	conjunction	joins two nouns (*Jack, Jill*)
Jill	noun	names a person
went	verb	expresses action
up	preposition	shows relationship of *went* to *hill*
hill	noun	names a thing
pail	noun	names a thing
of	preposition	shows relationship of *water* to *pail*
water	noun	names a thing
fell	verb	expresses action
down	preposition	shows relationship of *Jack* to *hill*
broke	verb	expresses action
his	pronoun	substitutes for noun *Jack's*
crown	noun	names a thing
came	verb	expresses action
after	preposition	shows relationship of *Jill* to *Jack*—she came *after* (him).

NOUNS

One of the chief difficulties in the spelling of nouns occurs in the formation of plurals. The following rules will help you to overcome these difficulties.

Regular Plurals

1. Most nouns form plurals by adding -s to the singular.

Singular	Plural
boy	boys
girl	girls
Greek	Greeks
home	homes
rib	ribs

2. Nouns ending in s, sh, z (or a z sound), ch, and x form plurals by adding -es.

	Singular	Plural
s	glass	glasses
	mass	masses
sh	flash	flashes
	crash	crashes
z	rose (z sound)	roses
	buzz	buzzes
ch	watch	watches
	match	matches
x	fox	foxes
	box	boxes

Exercise No. 7

Add -s or -es to each of the following singular nouns to form the correct plural. Rewrite the whole word in the blank space.

EXAMPLE: girl **girls**

a. tray
b. pie
c. ash
d. lynx
e. swan
f. wax
g. gnu
h. ostrich
i. kiss
j. snapper
k. grass
l. eel
m. albatross
n. moss
o. tax

How many of these nouns can you turn into adjectives?
EXAMPLE: *kiss* to *kissable.*

Irregular Plurals

(Rules affecting nouns and verbs ending in *y* are discussed in Chapter Ten under the heading "Final Silent Y.")

1. Nouns ending in **o**
Some nouns ending in **o** preceded by a **consonant** form plurals by adding -s; others form plurals by adding -es. The examples below are typical; learn them.

-s plurals	-es plurals
albinos	echoes
banjos	heroes
cantos	vetoes
zeros	potatoes
pianos	tornadoes

gauchos	tomatoes
altos	innuendoes
lassos	Negroes
dynamos	mosquitoes
tobaccos	torpedoes

All nouns ending in **o** preceded by a vowel form plurals by adding -s:

radios rodeos studios patios cameos

2. Nouns ending in **f**

Some nouns ending in -f (-fe, -ff) form plurals by adding -s; others change -f to -v and add -es. Study the examples below:

-s plurals

Singular	Plural
belief	beliefs
proof	proofs
fife	fifes
chief	chiefs
roof	roofs

-es plurals

Singular	Plural
loaf	loaves
thief	thieves
self	selves (also *themselves*)
wife	wives
life	lives

Exercise No. 8

Form the plurals of the following words:

a. silo
b. shelf
c. knife
d. calf
e. sheriff
f. rabbi
g. hoof
h. muff
i. embargo
j. gulf

3. Foreign nouns

Because most of these foreign nouns entered the English language late, they do not fall into the usual categories. Thus, they must simply be learned. Use your dictionary when in doubt.

Singular	Plural
addendum	addenda
agendum	agenda
alumnus	alumni (masculine)
alumna	alumnae (feminine)
analysis	analyses
apparatus	apparati (or apparatuses)
appendix	appendices (or appendixes)
axis	axes
basis	bases
crisis	crises
datum	data
formula	formulae (or formulas)
index	indices (or indexes)
memorandum	memoranda (or memorandums)
synopsis	synopses

Exercise No. 9

Each of the ten foreign nouns below is *plural*. Give the singular.

EXAMPLE: *synopses* is plural; *synopsis* is singular.

    a. radii (or radiuses)
    b. cherubim (or cherubs)
    c. virtuosi
    d. phenomena
    e. media
    f. vertebrae (or vertebras)
    g. dilettanti
    h. chateaux
    i. stigmata
    j. foci (or focuses)

4. Compound nouns

Generally, compound nouns form plurals by adding -s to the *more important* word.

Note that sometimes this word occurs first, sometimes last.

passers-by	brigadier **generals**
brothers-in-law	school**books**
attorneys-at-law	teaspoon**fuls**
commanders-in-chief	hand**fuls**
notaries public	pail**fuls**

5. Special nouns

Some nouns retain plural forms that are archaic—forms used in English up to about A.D. 1400.

Singular	Plural
ox	oxen
deer	deer
child	children
brother	brethren (or brothers)

Some nouns use the same form in both singular and plural: **barracks, goods, headquarters, measles, morals, pants, scissors, species, tactics, trousers.**

Exercise No. 10

A Review spelling test on Nouns. Before you take this test, review all the rules in this chapter. Your score on this test should be perfect before you proceed to the section on verbs.

a. What made those bright (flashs, flashes) in the northern sky?
b. Many nineteenth-century (Negroes, Negros) made important scientific contributions.
c. Where did you put the (scissor, scissors)?
d. Today's (agendum, agenda) contains several items that we must vote upon.
e. Is that particular piece of (data, datum) worth noting?
f. May I have three (teaspoonsful, teaspoonfuls) of sugar?
g. Standing on the corner watching (passerbys, passers-by) is my favorite recreation.

h. That cow has produced many (calves, calfs).

i. Our nation has placed (embargos, embargoes) on shipments to many foreign nations.

j. To our enormous (dynamoes, dynamos) we owe our improved electrical services.

k. Egotists attribute all virtues to (themselves, themselfs).

l. From atop the Eiffel Tower one can see across the (roofs, rooves) of Paris.

m. What is the latest news about the recently born (gnues, gnus) at the zoo?

n. Don't let children play with (matchs, matches).

o. Where are the little (foxes, foxen, foxs)?

p. The fox is harassing the (oxes, oxen).

q. Buy me three (loafs, loaves) of bread on your way home.

r. Three (wives, wifes) seem too much for any ordinary man.

s. Our daily lives are filled with too many minor (crisises, crises) to allow us the luxury of one really important crisis.

t. His last remarks seemed filled with unpleasant (innuendoes, innuendos).

VERBS

1. Regular and Irregular Verbs

Verbs are either **regular** or **irregular**, depending on the forms they use to show past time. **Regular** (or **weak**) verbs cause little spelling difficulty because they indicate past time by adding **-ed**, **-t**, or **-d** to the present form of the verb:

PRESENT	talk	feel	love
PAST	talked	felt	loved
PAST PARTICIPLE	talked	felt	loved

Irregular (or **strong**) verbs cause considerable difficulty because they show past time by varying a vowel within the present form of the verb:

PRESENT	sing	drink	know
PAST	sang	drank	knew
PAST PARTICIPLE	sung	drunk	known

Because irregular verbs are the ones most commonly used, you need to familiarize yourself with those most troublesome. Study the principal parts of the verbs in the list below, and then apply them in the exercise that follows.

PRESENT (INFINITIVE)	PAST	PAST PARTICIPLE
awake	awaked, awoke	awaked
be (am)	was	been
bear	bore	borne
begin	began	begun
bid	bade	bidden
break	broke	broken
burst	burst	burst
dive	dived, dove	dived
do	did	done
drink	drank	drunk
flee	fled	fled
fly	flew	flown
forsake	forsook	forsaken
get	got	got, gotten
go	went	gone
hang	hung, hanged	hung, hanged
have	had	had
know	knew	known
lay	laid	laid
lie	lay	lain
light	lit, lighted	lit, lighted
ring	rang	rung
rise	rose	risen
see	saw	seen
sing	sang	sung
slay	slew	slain
slink	slunk	slunk
speak	spoke	spoken
sting	stung	stung
stink	stank, stunk	stunk
swear	swore	sworn
swim	swam	swum

PRESENT (INFINITIVE)	PAST	PAST PARTICIPLE
wake	woke, waked	waked
wring	wrung	wrung
write	wrote	written

Exercise No. 11

Correct the errors in the verb form.
   EXAMPLE: The skunk stinked. *stank*
a. His boss fired him because he had drank so much while working.
b. The sun busted through from behind the clouds.
c. I could have swore I heard someone at the window.
d. I laid down all day yesterday but I still feel miserable.
e. After he had began his speech, the audience quickly lost interest.
f. The bee stang me on the nose.
g. I slayed many men, but Geoffrey has slewn many more.
h. I done what I could but he might have did a great deal more.
i. I awoked to the fact that my beloved had forsook me.
j. Do as you have been bade.

2. Singular and Plural Verbs

You can improve both your spelling and your grammar if you remember the following principles:

a. Verbs add -s to form the **singular.** Nouns use -s to form the **plural.**
b. Nouns acting as subjects of a sentence must agree with the verb in **number**—that is, if the noun is singular, the verb must be singular; if the noun is plural, the verb must be plural. Thus:
The dog (Singular noun subject) barks (Singular verb adds -s).
The dogs (Plural noun subject adds -s) bark (Plural verb).

Exercise No. 12

Which of the verbs in parentheses is correct?
a. One of these animals (attack, attacks) human beings.
b. Learning the rules of spelling often (confuses, confuse) me.
c. Candlelight and wine (adds, add) one touch of Venus.
d. Bill and Ed (was, were) expected for lunch.
e. The set of electric trains you wanted (has, have) been sold.
f. Each of us (suffers, suffer) when famine strikes.
g. Edwina is one of those muddleheaded girls who (need, needs) the guidance of a mature analyst.
h. Neither Gulliver nor his admirable friends (like, likes) those ugly creatures known as Yahoos.
i. Neither the principal nor the teacher (understands, understand) John's strange behavior.
j. Everybody here (knows, know) the importance of improving one's spelling.

Mastery Test Number 4

Do not proceed to the next chapter until you have taken this test. Master the spelling of these words from the **core list** before you try to learn those in the chapters ahead. Remember: in spelling your goal is a perfect score.

I. One of the core list words in each of the following sentences contains an *extra* letter that causes a misspelling. Remove the extra letter.

1. I should not like to emmbarrass my hostess by leaving too early.

2. Why do promminent financiers exaggerate their incomes to everyone except the Tax Bureau?
3. I cannot immagine a purple cow, and I have no desire to see one.
4. Some forreign words are familiar to everybody.
5. Red-headed girls often make a striking appearrance.

II. Choose the appropriate word for each blank. Note that in some instances, though all the parenthetic words are correctly spelled, only one is appropriate in context.
1. I have been (lead, led) by the nose till my feet feel like (lead, led).
2. What has (passed, past) between them is now (passed, past).
3. When I sought his (advice, advise), he refused to (advice, advise) me.
4. There is no (scents, sense) in acting like an animal simply because you find that a man of (principal, principle) cannot attain a (principle, principal) role in life.
5. If a child (various, varies) his habits frequently, his parents may have to try (various, varies) techniques to stabilize their offspring.

III. One word in each of the following groups is correctly spelled. Choose the word.
1. Attorneys seek an (apparant, apparent, apperant) flaw in their opponent's argument and then expose it.
2. Butlers (approch, approach, aproach) guests with extraordinary courtesy.
3. Cooks who create exotic new dishes become (heros, heroez, heroes) in the eyes of their employers.
4. Dentists have the mistaken notion that all pain is (immaginery, imaginery, imaginary).

5. Electricians need a vocabulary filled with words given them by (furriners, foreigners, foriegners): ampere, volt, watt, ohm, and the like.
6. Florists (persue, pursue, purrsue) weddings and funerals.
7. Geriatrists practice a form of medicine that seeks to deny the (prevalent, prevelent, prevelant) notion that the old have outworn their usefulness.
8. Horticulturists (analyse, analise, analyze) crops to determine the best ways to develop new strains of plants, fruits, and vegetables.
9. Icemen have been less (consistant, consisttent, consistent) in arriving on time since the refrigerator became popular.
10. Janitors often spend hours in the basement quietly listening to the (rythm, rhythmn, rhythm) of the oil burner.

IV. Proofread the following passages, correcting all errors in spelling.
A. Booker T. Washington, justifiably a herro to negros, applied his immagination and knowledge with such consistancy as to appear a man of herroic stature not only as a Negroe, but more important, as a man.
B. The beautiful herroine of Amazonian hieght but little gramar tryed several aproaches to achieve loveliness and literacy. Though she often trys studing her attempts at analisis of her strengths and weaknesses always fail.

SPECIAL WORD SECTION—MEDICINE

The words listed below appear frequently in articles about medicine as well as in books. Master their spelling; then test your knowledge of their *spelling* and *meaning* in the exercises that follow.

adenoids   epilepsy
allergy   hemorrhage
antibiotics   hormone
antiseptic   inoculate
antitoxin   laryngitis
astigmatism   obstetrics
cardiology   paralysis
catarrh   pediatrician
diagnosis   vaccine
eczema   virus

Special Word Exercise No. 4

Complete the following sentences by choosing the appropriate word from the list below. *If any word in the list is incorrectly spelled, correct it.*

I.

1. ...... is an inflammation of the mucous membrane of the nose.
2. A speaker whose ...... have swelled may sound as if he has ....
3. People who suffer from ...... to pollen or dust should live in ...... rooms.

larnygitis, addenoids, catarr, anteseptic, alergy

II.

1. Dr. Jones believes that the only good ...... is a dead one that has been converted into a ...... to prevent disease.
2. ...... are substances capable of destroying bacteria.
3. After the doctor's ...... revealed that she was pregnant, Mrs. Brown began to read articles about ....

antibioticks, virus, vacine, dignosis, obstetricks

III.

1. A ...... is more likely to treat a baby effectively than a podiatrist.
2. Injections of ...... extract often help to ease the skin irritation caused by ....
3. ...... will combat disease but it cannot prevent ...... of blood vessels.

hemorage, antitocksin, pediatrisian, ekzeema, horemon

IV.

1. If you have ......, you need glasses to reform the blurred images you now see.
2. Patients with heart ailments are treated by specialists in ....
3. To ...... one with the Salk vaccine practically assures immunity from infantile ....
4. ...... is known also as falling sickness.

cardiology, astigmitizm, innoculate, paralysis, epelipsy

CHAPTER SIX

AFFIXES: PREFIX AND SUFFIX

CORE LIST

arise	dominant	oppose
arising	efficient	opponent
character	efficiency	optimism
characteristic	exercise	precede
characterize	guidance	predominant
conceive	independence	prefer
conceivable	independent	preferred
consider	irrelevant	proceed
considerably	irresistible	procedure
convenience	irritable	refer
convenient	maintenance	referred
difference	operate	referring
different	opinion	
disappoint	opportunity	

Affixes are syllables added to the beginnings or endings of words. Specifically, affixes appear either as prefixes (syllables placed before the word—pre-fixed) or as suffixes (syllables appended to the end of the word). Used with discrimination and understanding—and spelled correctly—words built with prefixes and suffixes improve your ability to communicate effectively. In this chapter you will learn how to master the prefixes and suffixes that cause most difficulty in spelling. As you learn these prefixes and suffixes you will find innumerable words—beyond those on the core list and in the exercises—simpler to recognize, remember, and use.

PREFIXES

In the succeeding chapter, "Enjoying the Words You Spell," you will learn how to use prefixes to predict the meanings of words, to build whole families of words, and to qualify the meanings of words. Keep these vocabulary-building goals in mind as you begin to study the spelling aids given below. With practice you should acquire not only a better vocabulary, but one of whose spelling you are master.

The Major Pitfalls in Spelling with Prefixes

1. Because the last letter in certain prefixes is sometimes identical with the first letter in the root, you may become confused about whether a single or a double letter ought to be used. Which words in the following groups, for example, are correct?

A	B
disolve or dissolve	misspell or mispell
disatisfy or dissatisfy	misstep or mistep
dissagree or disagree	misschance or mischance

C

comerce or commerce
comit or commit
commpulsive or compulsive

43

Solution. Break the word into its component parts:

a. Write the prefix. *Memorize its spelling and meaning.*

dis- means "from, away, apart" (all in a negative sense)

mis- means "error, defect, wrong, badly"

com- means "together with"

b. Write the root word to which the prefix is to be affixed.

solve	spell
satisfy	step
agree	chance

merce (from Latin, **merx, mercis,** "merchandise")

mit (from Latin, **mittere,** "to send")

pulsive (from Latin, **pellere, pulsus,** "to beat")

c. Combine the prefix and the root. Note that the single or double letter depends solely on the accident of how root and prefix come together.

dissolve	mischance
dissatisfy	commerce
disagree	commit
misspell	compulsive
misstep	

Exercise No. 13

Which of the italicized words prefixed with **dis-, mis-,** or **com-** is incorrectly spelled? Use your dictionary when in doubt, and carefully note the meaning and origin of the root.

1. Berg's music often suffers from ugly *disonance.*
2. The hunchback of Notre Dame was *mishapen.*
3. Her skiing *misshap* laid her up for a week.
4. Sergeant Penn received a deserved *commendation* for his bravery.
5. Population increases in the metropolitan area *disuade* Max from moving back to civilization.
6. When Lou learned that his investments had failed, he was sorely *dissappointed.*
7. *Misprints* in the newspaper always disturb me.
8. Anyone who says that Gigli had a finer voice than Caruso is guilty of *mistatement.*
9. If you feel so strongly, why not write a letter to the *comissioner.*
10. Jerry is a *commpetent* worker, quite *dissimilar* from his shirking friend, Leonard.

2. Assimilation also causes difficulty. Our tongues normally seek the easiest way to pronounce any word. Consequently, many prefixes change from their original formation in order to merge more easily with— to **assimilate** with—roots. Thus, although prefix **com-,** which you have just learned, means "together with," it would look and sound ill if combined with **education** to form *comeducation.* Thus, your tongue— and your pen—drop the **m** to create **co-education.** No bank would ask you for *comlateral* on a loan; rather would they ask for **collateral.** The prefix *com-* here changes to **col-** to ease pronunciation.

Solution. Break the word into its component parts.

a. Write the prefix. Note whether it seems to be an assimilated form (A list of the most important assimilated prefix forms appears below).

b. Write the root word and then combine prefix and root.

Study the prefixes given below. They represent the most common sources of spelling problems resulting from assimilation.

PREFIX	TYPICAL WORDS
ad- (meaning "to, toward")	adhere, advertisement, adjudicate

a-	ascend, ascribe
ac-	accede, accord, accumulate
af-	affect, affix
al-	allot, allude, allocate
an-	annex, announce
ap-	apparent, applaud
ar-	arrive, arraign
as-	assist, assent, assemble, assign
at-	attendance, attest

dis- disturb, disease
(meaning "from, away," etc.)

di-	divert, digress, diligent
dif-	difference, differ, diffident, diffuse

in- intrude, invent, into, incline
(with verbs and nouns means "in, into, on")

il-	illuminate
im-	import, implore, imbibe
ir-	irrigate, irradiate

in- indecent, informal
(with adjectives means "not")

il-	illiterate, illegal, illicit
ig-	ignorant, ignoble
im-	immodest, immoral, improper
ir-	irregular, irrational

sub- submarine, submerge, submit
(meaning "under, beneath")

suc-	succumb, succinct
suf-	suffix, suffer
sug-	suggest
sup-	supplant
sus-	suspend, suspect, sustain

Exercise No. 14

Study the lists above before you do this exercise. Do not refer to the lists while you do it. Which word in parentheses is correctly spelled?

1. Keep to the point. Don't (digress, disgress).
2. The new dam will help (irigate, irrigate) the desolate wasteland.
3. Mother finally (sucumbed, succumbed) to my sister's entreaties.
4. Traitorousness is wholly (ilnoble, innoble, ignoble).
5. He (inbibes, imbibes) two quarts of milk per day.
6. Edwards was hired to (supplant, subplant) the ineffectual Williams.
7. More funds were (allocated, adlocated) for the new project.
8. The disputants agreed to have their differences (ajudicated, adjudicated).
9. The (submarine, sumarine) (sumerged, submerged).
10. Kay failed to note any (diference, difference) in her husband's attire.

3. Because certain prefixes are similarly spelled, you may confuse them. Which words in the following groups, for example, are correct?

Group A	Group B	Group C
prespire	discribe	antiroom
or	or	or
perspire	describe	anteroom
prevoke	dispise	antelabor
or	or	or
provoke	despise	antilabor

Solution. Break the word into its component parts.

a. Write the prefix. *Check its meaning in the dictionary.* Note that
 pre- means "before (in place or time)"
 per- means "through, throughout"
 pro- means "forward, in favor of"
 di- (dis-, dif-) means "away, apart, not"
 de- means "down"
 ante- means "before"
 anti- means "against"

b. Combine the appropriate prefix with the root. Thus:

When you **perspire**, you "breathe" (**spire**) "through" (**per-**) your pores.

When you **provoke** someone, you "call" (**vok**) "forward" (**pro-**) his resentment.

When you **describe** someone, you "write" (**scribe**) "down" (**de-**) your observation.

When you **despise** someone, you "look" (**spise**) "down" (**de-**) on him.

When you wait in an **anteroom**, you wait in the room "before" (**ante-**) the main room.

When you are **antilabor**, you are "against" (**anti-**) labor.

Exercise No. 15

Choose the appropriate word within the parentheses.

1. Pronouns must agree with their (anti-cedents, antecedents) in number, gender, and person.
2. Why must Eric (presist, persist) in acting so unpleasantly?
3. Edwige refused to (divulge, devulge) the whereabouts of her secret files.
4. A good (anteseptic, antiseptic) will cleanse that wound.
5. The letter *i* (precedes, procedes) the let-ler *j*.
6. If you cannot answer the question ask your (professor, prefessor, perfessor).
7. I know of no (antedote, antidote) for love sickness.
8. But lack of taste is a remediable (desease, disease).
9. The (description, discription) of Public Enemy #5 is on file at Headquarters.
10. Whatever the grimness of the outlook, I shall not (dispair, despair).

SUFFIXES

In the next chapter you will learn how to benefit from the fact that suffixes alter the *meaning* of a word and affect its *grammatical function*. First, however, you must cope with some of the spelling problems raised by suf-fixes.* Most serious among these difficulties is the spelling of a vowel in an unaccented suf-fix. How, for example, would you spell the fol-lowing words?

extravagant or extravagent
innocant or innocent
detestable or destestible
radiance or radience
existance or existence
irresistable or irresistible

The troublespots in these words may be broken down to a few groups of suffixes; learn the prin-ciples governing their usage and you should be able to reduce the number of errors you commit in spelling.

-Ant, -ent, -ancy, -ency.

-Ant and **-ent** serve as endings for either *ad-jectives* or *nouns*. Both suffixes mean the same —"an agent" (noun), a "quality" (adjective). Both suffixes sound the same. The result—a spelling problem.

-Ance and **-ence** serve as endings only for *nouns*. Both suffixes mean the same—"action, state, quality." Both suffixes sound the same. The result once more is a spelling problem.

Solution: -ance and -ant

1. Think of a *related* word. Thus, when puz-zling about **radiance** or **radiant**, think of *radiate*. If the suffix in the related word has an **a**, the suffix in the problem word will probably be **-ant** or **-ance: radiant, radiance.**

---

* Only certain major points about suffixes are discussed in this chapter. When you have mastered these, study the other principles involving spelling with suffixes. These appear in Chapters Ten and Eleven.

Note these further examples:

	Related word
dominance	dominate
tolerance	tolerate
hesitance	hesitate

2. When in doubt, consult the dictionary under *both* endings.

Solution: -ence and -ent

1. If the root ends in **soft c** or **soft g**, the suffix will probably be **-ence** or **-ent**. Thus, if the root is **innoc** (soft c) the word should be spelled **innocence** (**innocent**).

Note these further examples:

intelligence	(soft g)
magnificent	(soft c)
negligent	(soft g)

HINT: Roots ending in **hard c** or **hard g** are infrequent: signicance, extravagant.

2. If the root ends in **-sist** or **-xist**, the suffix will probably be **-ence** or **-ent**. Thus, **existence**. Note these further examples:

consistent
insistent
persistence

HINT: **Resistance** is an exception.

3. If in its original form as verb the word:

   a. Takes an accent on the final syllable
   b. Ends with **r** preceded by a vowel

Then the noun suffix should be **-ence** or **-ent**

For example: **confer** is a verb

   a. accented on the final syllable—con-fer'
   b. ending with **r** preceded by the vowel **e**

Therefore, to change **confer** into a noun, add the suffix **-ence—conference**

HINT: The fact that the noun may undergo a shift in accent—**con**'ference—does not affect the spelling.

Note these similar examples:

refer'	reference
prefer'	preference
defer'	deference

Exercise No. 16

Add the appropriate suffix: **-ant, -ent, -ance, -ence** to the incomplete words.

EXAMPLE: Jonas is a persist.... fellow.
Ans. persistent

1. Adoles.... is a stage of development that begins at twelve and sometimes ends.
2. One hundred and fifty dollars a month is not sufficient for subsist.....
3. The autocrat of the dinner table brooked no interfer.....
4. Are you always this ignor...., or only when you think?
5. The lawyer's demands for alimony were extravag.....
6. Baritones often have reson.... voices.
7. What infer.... do you derive from his statements?
8. I am toler.... of all except those whom I hate.
9. Why are you hesit.... about accepting his offer?
10. The librarian will help you locate the refer.... volume you need.

-able, -ible

Both suffixes serve as endings for adjectives.
Both suffixes mean the same—"capable, able to."
Both suffixes sound the same.
The result—a spelling problem.

Solution:

1. Think of a related word, preferably a *noun* ending in -ation or -ition (or its derivatives -tion, -ion, -sion).

   EXAMPLE:

   a. If the related noun ends with -ation, the adjective suffix will probably be -able. Thus, when deciding between *inflammable* and *inflammible*, think of inflammation. Since the noun uses the suffix, -ation, the adjective will be **inflammable**.

   b. If the related noun ends with -ition or one of its variants, the adjective suffix will probably be -ible. When deciding between *reducible* and *reducable*, think of reduction. Since the noun uses the suffix -tion, the adjective will be **reducible**.

Note the following typical examples:

-able	*Related words*
admirable	admiration
demonstrable	demonstration
imaginable	imagination
durable	duration
navigable	navigation

-ible	*Related words*
admissible	admission
collectible	collection
corruptible	corruption
reducible	reduction
convertible	conversion

HINT: Here is an exception to memorize: **predictable**. Its related word, contrary to the rule above, is **prediction**.

2. If the root is itself a *full word* (or lacks only a *final e*), the suffix is usually -able. Note the following examples:

Full word	*Full word, lacking final e*
detestable	excitable (excite)
creditable	sizable (size)

dependable	admirable (admire)
eatable	desirable (desire)
laughable	movable (move)

If the root is not a full word, the suffix is usually -ible. Note the following:

irresistible	possible
eligible	terrible
audible	horrible
plausible	responsible
visible	invincible

3. If the root ends in **hard c** or **hard g**, the suffix will probably be -able.

despicable	explicable
extricable	amicable
navigable	

If the root ends in **soft c** or **soft g**, the suffix will probably be -ible.

reducible	incorrigible
legible	forcible
irascible	

HINT: Because -able occurs four times as frequently as -ible, you should—if you cannot apply the rules above or get to a dictionary—use -able as the more likely suffix. But use this hint only as an emergency device, not as your usual method.

Exercise No. 17

Add the appropriate suffix— -able or -ible— to the incomplete words. If any changes need be made in the final spelling of the root word, make them.

1. With the aid of modern medicine leprosy is now a cur.... disease.
2. All values cannot be material; one must have faith in the intang.... as well.
3. Mighty Moe stood forth as the invinc.... conqueror of all.

4. Your failure to pass geometry after three terms is deplor.....
5. One cannot hold the criminally insane entirely blam.....
6. His arguments are rarely plaus.....
7. Mr. Grump stormed into the office, as irasc.... as ever.
8. Mr. Jolly beamed at his employees, as amic.... as ever.
9. Your arguments are ultimately reduc.... to one central point.
10. Can you provide me with demonstr.... proof of this theory?
11. Many stars are vis.... on clear nights.
12. The ultimate day of man's doom is not predict.....
13. Speak louder. You are inaud.....
14. Your excuses are thoroughly accept.....
15. I remain immov.... despite your pleas.

MISCELLANEOUS MISCHIEF MAKERS

If you have mastered the suffixes already given, you should have gained control over a major weakness in spelling. The suffixes which follow—though bothersome—cause less difficulty. Nevertheless, study them and familiarize yourself with the words that illustrate their use.

1. **-Ise, ize,** and **-yze** (meaning "to use a process, to bring into being")

Most verbs using this suffix end in **-ize:**

harmonize	legalize
pasteurize	realize
recognize	criticize

Several verbs, however, use **-ise:**

surprise	arise
despise	exercise
advertise	lengthwise
supervise	advise
disguise	compromise
enterprise	crosswise

Rarely do verbs end in **-yze. Analyze** and **paralyze** are the two most common.

2. **-Or** and **-er** (meaning "one who does or performs")

Most nouns using this suffix end in **-or** (especially words of Latin origin):

elevator	counselor
advisor	distributor
aviator	professor
competitor	accelerator
senator	

Several nouns, however (especially those of English origin), end in **-er:**

pusher	teacher
maker	prisoner
officer	doer
writer	foreigner

3. **-Efy** and **-ify** (meaning "to make, to cause to be")

Almost all verbs using this suffix end in **-ify:**

magnify	beautify
testify	classify
mortify	

Rarely do verbs end in **-efy: liquefy** and **rarefy** are the two most common.

4. **-Ly** and **-ally** (meaning "the manner of doing")

Words ending in l add the adverbial suffix **-ly:**

especially	hopefully
skillfully	finally
accidentally	harmfully
truthfully	naturally
really	meaningfully

HINT: Words ending in **double l** drop one l, then add the suffix **-ly: dull** becomes dul ly **dully.**

Add **-ally** only when the word ends in **-ic:**

automatically	emphatically
basically	mathematically

Exercise No. 18

Choose the appropriate suffix needed to complete the root word.

EXAMPLE: Is George a farm . . . . . (-er, -or)?

Ans. *farmer*

1. That child deserves to be chast.... (-ised, -ized).
2. Forgive us our debts as we forgive our debt.... (-ers, -ors).
3. Can you liqu.... (-efy, -ify) steel?
4. Dev.... (-ise, -ize) me a scheme to popularize mushrooms.
5. Do you think the consum.... (-or, -er) market will respond to mushroom soup?
6. These new hormones beaut.... (-efy, -ify) even my dog's complexion.
7. Don't critic.... (-ize, -ise) my wife's hair. At least it's hers.
8. Does the average man like his employ.... (-or, -er)?
9. I cannot real.... (-y, -ly) get accustomed to your face.

10. I recogn.... (-ise, -ize) the street where you live.
11. Ask the Senat.... (-er, -or) from New York to rise.
12. I suspect that basic.... (-ly, -ally) your motives are dishonest.
13. Did you push that hatpin in brother's coat accident.... (-ally, -ly)?
14. I can't truthful.... (-y, -ly) say why I think as I do.
15. Will John test.... (-efy, -ify) against his sister?

Mastery Test Number 5

Do not proceed to the next chapter until you have taken this test. Master the spelling of these words from the **core list** before you try to learn those in the chapters ahead. Remember: in spelling your goal is a perfect score.

I. Each of the core list words in the following sentences either A: *Needs an extra letter;* B: *Has an extra letter.* In either case correct the spelling.

1. The boxer's oponent outweighed him by twenty-five pounds.
2. In my oppinion, your taste in hats is absurd.
3. Will you excercise your right to vote at the trustee's meeting?
4. How would you charcterize a man who beats his children but not his horse?
5. I will not disapoint you by being present at your next party.
6. We should have prefered that Alfred not leave school before finishing.
7. What proceedure ought I follow in acquiring my visa?
8. No real diference separates identical twins.
9. Her charms I find irresistible, her friends less so.

10. All arguments that disagree with mine I dismiss as irelevant.

II. One word in each of the following groups is correctly spelled. Choose the word.

1. To whom have you (referred, refered, refferred) your maid?
2. I think it (conceiveable, conceivable, concievable) that oysters appear in June.
3. Which (charcteristic, charactaristic, characteristic) of the mosquito did you list in your notes?
4. Correct spelling is a necessity not a (convenience, conveneince, convennience).
5. Typing (efficeincy, efficiency, efficiancy) increases with practice.
6. The investors looked at the rising prices as a cause for (optimmism, optimism, optimasm).
7. Why do some women get (iritable, irritable, irritible) when you tell them the truth?
8. The (maintainance, maintenence, maintenance) expenses for a motor-boat are high.
9. I have grown (considerably, consideribly, considerrably) older since we last met.
10. Every modern high school has a (guidence, giudance, guidance) department to help young people select an appropriate vocation.

III. Match the core list word with the appropriate context. If the core list word is misspelled, correct it.

EXAMPLE: Where are they eating tonight?

dinning
flying
shooting

Ans. dining

Column A

1. I'm against it
2. Will you get up?
3. They are simply unalike
4. He works effectively
5. He has a strong personality
6. Your chance has come
7. I find it most handy
8. I want my freedom
9. What happened before?
10. Can you describe his personality?

Column B

a. convenient
b. independance
c. preceed
d. diferant
e. efficeincy
f. dominant
g. arrise
h. charcter
i. opose
j. opporttunity

IV. Proofread the following passage, correcting all errors in spelling.

An independant man preferrs to consider his own thinking as valid. He refuses to reffer to the perdomminant pattern of the mob for a course to follow. Perhaps he may concieve that the mob—referring to mass thinking—operates automatically, their behavior arrising from body sensation and proseeding to thoughtless motion.

SPECIAL WORD SECTION— PHYSICS AND MATHEMATICS

The following words appear frequently in popular articles about physics and mathematics as well as in books. Master their spelling; then test your knowledge of their *spelling* and *meaning* in the exercises that follow.

abacus	fidelity
amplifier	hypotenuse
angle	infinity
cathode ray	integer
circumference	isosceles
cosmic ray	nuclear fission
cyclotron	numerator
decimal	perpendicular
denominator	quotient
electronics	supersonic

Special Word Exercise No. 5

Complete the following sentences by choosing the appropriate word from the list below. *If any word in the list is incorrectly spelled, correct it.*

I.

1. A more popular expression for ...... is "splitting the atom."
2. A ...... can produce atomic projectiles whose energy exceeds a hundred million volts.
3. A sensitive ...... improves the ...... of recorded music.
4. Television images are made up of electrons beamed by a ....

    fidellity   cathode ray   cycletron
     amplifeir   nooclear fishon

II.

1. ...... enter our atmosphere from outer space.
2. ...... aircraft travel at 738 mph, exceeding the speed of sound.
3. An ...... would be of little help in computing sums ranging up to ....
4. ...... is the branch of physics that studies the characteristics of electrons.

    infinnity   suppersonic   electronics
      abbacus   cosmick rays

III.

1. A whole number is an ......; any tenth part of a whole number is a ....
2. When writing fractions, place above the line the ......, below the line the ....
3. The number obtained when one quantity is divided by another is a ....

    decimal   demonator   quoteint
      numerator   integer

IV.

1. Is it simpler to find the ...... of a circle or the ...... of an ...... triangle?
2. The side of a right-angled triangle opposite the right angle is called the ....
3. A man standing erect is ...... to the floor on which he stands.

    angel   circumferance   hypotenoose
      isosceles   perpandiculer

CHAPTER SEVEN

ENJOYING THE WORDS YOU SPELL:
AFFIXES AND VOCABULARY

CORE LIST

aggressive	original	summed
arguing	philosophy	suppose
argument	propaganda	suppress
control	propagate	technique
controlled	psychoanalysis	temperament
fulfill	psychopathic	therefore
further	ridicule	together
hindrance	ridiculous	tragedy
humor	sergeant	tyranny
humorist	satire	unusual
humorous	satirize	unusually
hypocrisy	sophomore	villain
hypocrite	subtle	
origin	summary	

You wish to spell correctly for several good reasons. One especially good reason is to allow yourself an opportunity to increase your vocabulary. At this point, armed with the affixes you should now have mastered, you may find it worthwhile to learn how roots, prefixes, and suffixes can help you to improve your vocabulary as well as your spelling.*

ROOTS AND YOUR VOCABULARY

Roots contain the organic structure of a word. They are the heart of vocabulary building because they pump meaning into the word.

* (Material for this chapter has been adapted from Chapters 4, 5, 6 of *Word Mastery Made Simple* by Arthur Waldhorn and Arthur Zeiger, with permission.)

Consider, for example, the following group of words:

fact factory factor faction factotum

Each of these words has in common the Latin root **fac**, meaning "make" or "do." Thus a **fact** is "that which is already *done*" (deed, act); a **factory** "a place where things are *made*" (a plant where items are manufactured); a **factor** "one who *does* or *makes* things for someone else" (a merchant, an agent), or, in another sense, "some *fact* that *makes* things what they are" (circumstance, condition); a **faction** is a clique that *does* things together" (partisan group); and a **factotum** "an all-around man hired *to do* all sorts of jobs" (a handyman).

In each word the root **fac** provides the core of meaning: the root is the heart that pumps meaning into the word. The single root **fac** produces more than one hundred English words. You can combine with other roots: add **simile** (like) and you get **facsimile**, "that which is made like something else," or "a reproduction"; add **manu** (hand), and your new word is **manufacture**, "that which is made by hand." A bit further in this chapter you will learn how roots can be combined with prefixes to form words, but first you should learn the five roots (and their variants) given below. Among the most common roots in English, these occur in hundreds of words. Once you master them, you will be able to build whole families of words. (See top of next page.)

ROOT	MEANING	TYPICAL WORDS (Add others of your own)
mit (Latin)	send, throw	permit, transmit, omit, submit
miss		mission, omission, submission, emissary
mise		promise, demise, surmise
cap (Latin)	take, hold	capture, capable, captivate, capacity
cip		anticipate, principal, participate
cept		accept, deception, concept
ten (Latin)	hold	tenure, tenant, tenacious, lieutenant
tent		content, detention
tin		imminent, incontinent, pertinent
tain		abstain, pertain, maintain
auto (Greek)	self	autobiography, automatic, autocrat, autonomous, autopsy
log (Greek)	word, speech, science	logic, logarithm, epilogue, prologue, psychology, catalogue, eulogy

Exercise No. 19

Give the meaning of the **root** in each of the following italicized words. What is the meaning of the word in context?

EXAMPLE: A dangerous *faction*. The root is *fac* meaning "make" or "do." In the context of the phrase, *faction* means "a clique of partisans whose actions may cause trouble."

1. An American *emissary*
2. A *tenacious* grip
3. An *untenable* argument
4. An unhappy *demise*
5. A false *surmise*
6. A guided *missile*
7. A heartfelt *eulogy*
8. An *autonomous* state
9. An *incontinent* drunkard
10. A willful *autocrat*

PREFIXES AND YOUR VOCABULARY

Prefixes are not nearly so numerous as roots but they are vitally important in building vocabulary. Here are some of the ways in which they will help you.

1. Building Word Families

Like roots, prefixes serve to build whole families of words. You know now, for example, that the Latin root **fac** means "make" or "do." When you combine certain prefixes with that root (or its variants) you can build innumerable words:

Combine prefix **af-** (to) with root **fect** (variant of *fac*)—**affect**, "to do to, to influence"

Combine prefix **bene-** (good, well) with **fac**; add the suffix **-or** (one who)—**benefactor**, "one who does good"

How would you explain the function of the prefix in these similarly related words: **effect, confection, infect, disinfect, coefficient?**

As you increase your supply of prefixes, you will be able to combine words more readily. On page 51 are three common prefixes—listed with their assimilated forms. Add them to those you have already learned.

PREFIX	MEANING	TYPICAL WORDS (Add others of your own)
ad- (Latin)	to, toward	advertisement, adhere, adjudicate
a-		ascribe, averse
ac-		accord, accede, accumulate
af-		affect, affix, affiance
ag-		aggravate, aggrandize, aggregate
al-		allocate, allot, allude
as-		assist, assemble, assent
at-		attendance, attest, attenuate
ex- (Latin)	out, from, away	expatriate, external, expatiate
e-		educate, evoke, eliminate, elongate
ef-		efficient, effect, efficacious
syn- (Greek)	with, together	synagogue, syntax, synthesis, synonym
sym-		sympathy, symphony, symmetry
syl-		syllable, syllogism

Exercise No. 20

Select the syllables that logically complete the following prefixes.

EXAMPLE: The priest offered the widow sym-.... (phony, *pathy*, metry)

1. Words identical in meaning are syn.... (tax, agogue, onyms).
2. Tyrants seek to ag.... (gravate, grandize, gregate) their power.
3. Americans who stay abroad are ex.... (patriots, patriates, patiates).
4. The judge sought to ad.... (judicate, monish, here) the labor dispute.
5. His practical solutions were always ef.... (ficacious, fulgent, fusive).

2. Qualifying Word Meaning

Prefixes help you to discriminate among words because they *qualify* the meanings of words to which they are attached. The Latin root **cursor**, for example, means "runner." The Latin prefix **pre-** of course means "before." A precursor means literally "something or someone who runs before." In its current sense, **precursor** means "a forerunner, a sign foretelling what is to come." Or, again, the Greek root **arche** means "government, leader"; the Greek prefix **an-** means "not." Anarchy, therefore, means "without government, or without a leader."

In each of these words the prefix *qualifies* the meaning of the root. A word of caution: Avoid the assumption that the formula "root plus prefix" always gives a meaningful sum. Combining the Latin root **ole** ("to smell") with the Latin prefix **re-** ("back") gives redolent, meaning literally "to smell back." In current usage, however, **redolent** sometimes means "fragrant," but more generally it is used figuratively to mean "suggestive of or imbued with a tone or quality," as "The ancient desk in the corner of his study was **redolent** of the serene hours of his boyhood."

Even though you must avoid hasty conclusions, your study of relationships between roots and prefixes will appreciably help your progress.

Exercise No. 21

Give the *negative* form of each of the following words. Use those prefixes which mean "not, away, from, apart." Use each word in a sentence.

> EXAMPLE: firm—infirm; limit—delimit; able—unable

The infirm man had difficulty ascending the hill.

a. enchant
b. honorable
c. ethical
d. literate
e. fallible
f. rational
g. agree
h. conduct
i. quiet
j. engage

SUFFIXES AND YOUR VOCABULARY

Suffixes always signify a part of speech. Recall, for example, those you have already learned:

Verb suffixes:
-ate
-ise, -ize, -yze
-efy, -ify

Noun suffixes:
-ation, -ition
-er, -or
-ance, -ence
-ant, -ent

Adjective suffixes:
-able, -ible
-ic
-ant, -ent

Adverb suffixes:
-ly, -ally

Learn to recognize these signs, what they mean, how they function. You will find your knowledge immensely valuable in putting suffixes to work. Here is how you can do it:

1. Make your verbs serve also as nouns and adjectives.
   Drop the verb suffix; add to the root a noun suffix.

culminate (verb) minus -ate (verb suffix) plus -ation (noun suffix) equals culmination (noun)

abominate (verb) minus -ate plus -able (adjective suffix) equals abominable (adjective)

If the verb is *whole*, to form either noun or adjective, add the appropriate suffix.

noun: till (verb) plus -er equals tiller (noun)

adjective: sing (verb) plus -able equals singable (adjective)

Exercise No. 22

Change each of the following verbs into a noun or an adjective, or, where possible, each.

Use each in a sentence.

a. hypnotize
b. comprehend
c. equivocate
d. liquefy
e. criticize
f. navigate
g. certify
h. analyze
i. mechanize
j. effervesce

2. Make your nouns serve also as verbs and adjectives.
   Drop the noun suffix; add to the root a verb suffix.

navigation (noun) minus **-ation** (noun suffix) plus **-ate** (verb suffix) equals **navigate** (verb)

certification (noun) minus **-ation** plus **-able** (adjective suffix) equals **certifiable** (adjective)

If the noun is *whole*, to form either adjective or verb, add the appropriate suffix.

verb: system (noun) plus -ize equals systematize (the original root is *systema*).

adjective: artist (noun) plus -ic equals artistic.

Exercise No. 23

Change each of the following nouns into a verb or adjective. Use each in a sentence.

a. apprehension
b. liberation
c. consummation
d. diffidence
e. medication
f. admiration
g. ignition
h. malice
i. gratuity
j. regulation

3. Make your adjectives serve also as verbs, nouns, and adverbs.

Drop the adjective suffix; add to the root a noun suffix.

barbaric (adjective) minus **-ic** (adjective suffix) plus **-an** (noun suffix) equals **barbarian** (noun)

precipitous (adjective) minus **-ous** (adjective suffix) plus **-ate** (verb suffix) equals **precipitate** (verb)

Form the adverb by adding **-ly** to the adjective: **maniacally, efficiently, diametrically, superficially, hopelessly.**

Exercise No. 24

Change each of the following adjectives into a verb, noun, or adverb. Use each in a sentence.

a. categorical
b. hypothetical
c. materialistic
d. paternal
e. facetious

Mastery Test Number 6

Do not proceed to the next chapter until you have taken this test. Master the spelling of the words from the **core list** before you try to learn those in the chapters ahead. Remember: in spelling your goal is a perfect score.

I. Match the core list word with the appropriate context. If the core list word is misspelled, correct it.

Column A

1. The unfortunate man is mad
2. The doctor uses Freud's methods
3. He has an amusing cast of mind
4. The hero dies at the end
5. He pretends to be what he is not
6. His reasoning is deft and ingenious
7. What sort of disposition has he?
8. He is a despicable fellow
9. A concise statement
10. A student in his second year at school

Column B

a. humor
b. hyppocrite
c. temprament
d. villian
e. sophmore
f. psycopathic
g. phycoanalysis
h. suptle
i. tradgedy
j. summery

II. One word in each of the following groups is correctly spelled. Choose the word.

1. A cogent (arguement, argument, arrgument) is always persuasive.
2. Dress designers forever seek fresh, (orriginel, originel, original) patterns.
3. I have never found slapstick particularly (humerous, humorous, humorus).
4. (Hypocracy, Hypocrisy, Hypocricy) is an homage vice pays to virtue.
5. On what ground work of knowledge have you built your (philosophy, pholosophy, filosophy)?
6. In the kitchen most husbands are more (hinderance, hindrence, hindrance) than help.

7. Why do you mock and (redicule, ridecule, ridicule) that poor but honest fool?

8. (Sattire, Satire, Sattere) exposes man's foibles and laughs at them.

9. Your acute observation (summed, sumed, sunned) up my feelings precisely.

10. Tyrants attempt to (surpress, suppress, supress) popular expression of opinion.

III. One of the core list words in each of the following sentences needs an *extra* letter to make it correct. Add the necessary letter.

1. I have controled my temper too long.
2. Down with tyrany. Long live democracy.
3. A peaceful man restrains his agressive tendencies.
4. Supose then that I were in your place.
5. What an unusal way to eat peas—with a straw.
6. New tecniques for increasing reading speed are available now for all.
7. What is needed therefor is a good five cent candy bar.
8. Usually he is late, but tonight he is unusualy so.
9. Someday we may have a television humrist who is truly comic.
10. Why do Army privates always have such strong feelings about their sergants?

IV. Proofread the following passage, correcting all spelling errors.

Futher argueing about how their government propegates properganda seems rediculous. We must realize that their properganda does fullfil its purpose—to control men's minds. Our best means of retaliation is to work toggether, to expose the orrigin of such thinking, and finally to satirise the men who foist it upon the people.

SPECIAL WORD SECTION— ART, MUSIC, DANCE

The words listed below appear frequently in newspaper reviews and articles about art, music, and dance. Often they are misspelled. Master their spelling; then test your knowledge of their *spelling* and *meaning* in the exercise that follows.

abstraction	dissonance
a capella	entrechat
arabesque	fugue
atonality	gouache
ballet	madrigal
cadence	pirouette
ceramic	rhapsody
chiaroscuro	staccato
choreography	surrealism
counterpoint	symphony

Special Word Exercise No. 6

Complete the following sentences by choosing the appropriate word from the list below. *If any word is incorrectly spelled, correct it.*

I.

1. Lovers of ......—the union of dance, mime, and music—attend most carefully to ......, the arrangement of steps in dance movement.

2. The ...... keeps the dancer on one toe; the ...... on one foot; and the ...... off the ground altogether.

    arebesque   balet   choreography
    entrechatte   pihouette

II.

1. In art ...... avoids photographic accuracy or any form of outward reality.

2. ...... uses symbols and psychic association as the core for its painting.

3. The technique of painting with opaque watercolor is known as . . . .
4. The distribution of light and dark in a painting is known as . . . .
5. . . . . . . art uses clay and other earth materials to shape exquisite decorative forms.

   chirascuro abstraction ceramick
   surealism guoache

III.

1. Bach's D Minor . . . . . . relies on . . . . . . to achieve its concise symmetry.
2. The . . . . . . usually employs secular themes whereas the motet—also a choral work—uses sacred themes.
3. Above all else, a . . . . . . should develop a theme during its four movements.

4. The appeal of a . . . . . . is akin to that of free verse—both have the freshness of improvisation.

   synphony madragal fuggue
   rapsody counterpoint

IV.

1. Composers who ignore the conventional tones of music strive for . . . . . .; often they achieve merely . . . .
2. Unaccompanied choral singing—originally performed in chapels—is called . . . .
3. When the score calls for a transition from a flowing . . . . . to . . . . . ., the conductor's arms will make short, rapid motions to indicate the beat.

   a capella attonality cadense
   disonnance stacatto

Do not proceed to the next chapter until you have taken these Halfway Tests. The words in Part I have been selected from the **core list** of words *you have already studied. You should achieve a perfect score on this test.* If you do not, review the principles discussed in the preceding chapters and continue to study until you attain perfection. Remember, spelling mastery is what you are after. No compromise with perfection will do. That is a weakness you must not allow yourself.

Part I: Underline the one correctly spelled word in each of the following groups.

1. loseing, loosing, losing, lossing
2. proceed, procede, proseed, prosede
3. oppinion, opinion, opinnion, oppinnion
4. writing, writeing, writting, writteing
5. proffessor, profesor, proffesor, professor
6. exsistence, existance, existence, exsistance
7. foriegn, forein, forien, foreign
8. busyness, bussiness, business, bussyness
9. conveneince, convenience, convennience, convinience
10. efficeincy, eficiency, efficciency, efficiency
11. argument, arguement, argumment, argumint
12. redicule, ridicule, riddicule, reddicule
13. marraige, marridge, marriage, marrage
14. conscientous, conscientus, conscientious, consceintious
15. concievible, concievable, conceivible, conceivable
16. tradgedy, tradegy, tragedy, tradgidy
17. hieght, height, hiegth, heighth
18. prevelent, prevalent, prevelant, prevellant
19. benifited, benefitted, benefited, benifeted
20. refered, refferred, reffered, referred
21. immaginary, imaginary, imaggiery, imaginery
22. phychology, psycology, psychology, pshychology
23. therefore, therefor, therefour, therfore
24. enviroment, enviorment, environment, enviornment
25. beleif, beleaf, belief, bellief
26. maintainence, maintenence, maintainance, maintenance
27. intrepation, interpertation, interpretation, interpatation
28. experiance, expereince, experience, experrience
29. dissappoint, disapoint, disappoint, dissapoint
30. precede, preceed, preseed, presede
31. embarrass, emmbarass, embaras, embarass
32. begining, beggining, beginning, begginning
33. disasterous, disastarous, disastterous, disastrous
34. disatisfied, dissatisfied, dissatisfyed, disatisfyed
35. hypicrit, hypocrit, hypocrite, hypokrite
36. criticise, critticise, criticize, critticize
37. occassion, ocassion, occasion, occazion
38. rythm, rhthm, ryhthm, rhythm
39. atheletic, atletic, athletic, athletick
40. independance, independence, independince
41. comparative, comparitive, compareative, compareitive
42. benificial, benefishal, beneficial, benefical
43. oportunity, opportunity, oppertunity, opertunity
44. intrest, interrest, intterest, interest
45. exaggerate, exagerate, exsagerate, exaggarate
46. hypocricy, hypocracy, hypocrisy, hypokricy

60

47. diferent, different, differant, diferant
48. irritible, iritable, irrittable, irritable
49. temperment, temprement, temperament, temprament
50. effective, afective, efective, effactive

Part II: Underline the one correctly spelled word in each of the following groups.

The following words have been taken from exercises 1-24.

1. strengh, strength, strenkth, strenth
2. amicable, amicible, amickible, amiccable
3. anticedent, antecedant, antecedent, anticedant
4. Artic, Arctick, Arctic, Artick
5. background, backround, backgrond, backrund
6. boyant, buoyent, buoyant, bouyant
7. temprature, temparature, tempereture, temperature
8. calves, calfs, callves, calfes
9. chastize, chastise, chestize, chestise
10. chatow, chateau, cheteau, chatoe
11. chocolit, choclate, chocolat, chocolate
12. collitch, colledge, college, collidge
13. comissioner, commissioner, commisionar, comisioner
14. competent, competant, compatent, compitent
15. consumate, consummit, consummate, consumit
16. krisis, crisis, crissis, crysis
17. cureable, curable, currable, curible
18. demonstrible, demmonstrable, demonstrable, demonstrouble
19. deplorable, deploreable, deplorrable, deplorible
20. dispair, despear, despare, despair
21. divulge, devulge, divvulge, divuldge
22. diery, diarry, diary, dierry
23. difidant, diffident, diffidant, difident
24. degress, diggress, digress, deggress
25. dilettante, dilletante, dilitante, dilettente
26. dinamo, dynammo, dynamo, dynnamo
27. eficacious, efficcacious, efficacious, efficashious
28. embargo, emmbargo, embergo, emborgo
29. eggsactly, exactly, exsactly, exectly
30. frevolous, frivollous, frivolous, frivlous
31. gratuitous, gratutous, gratuitious, gratitus
32. hesitent, hessitant, hessitent, hesitant
33. iggurent, ignerent, ignorant, ignerant
34. illiterate, illitrate, iliterate, illitarete
35. imovable, immovable, immoveable, immovible
36. inuendo, innuendo, innueindo, innuindo
37. invincible, invincable, invinceible, invinceable
38. knifes, knives, nifes, nives
39. liquify, liquefy, liquefye, liquifie
40. mathmatics, mathamatics, mathcmatics, mathematicks
41. miniture, minniature, miniature, minieture
42. misterious, mysterious, mystrious, mysterius
43. parlement, parliment, parliamant, parliament
44. plausable, plausible, plawsible, plasible
45. recognize, reconize, recognise, recoggnize
46. reducable, reducible, reduceible, reduceable
47. referance, refference, reference, referrence
48. sissors, skissors, scissors, scissers
49. shelfs, shelvs, shelfes, shelves
50. sucumb, succomb, succumb, sucomb

CHAPTER EIGHT

LEARNING THE RULES: APOSTROPHES AND CAPITALS

CORE LIST

academic	basically	discipline
academically	basis	doesn't
academy	Britain	etc.
accept	Britannica	familiar
acceptable	challenge	finally
acceptance	Christ	fundamental
accepting	Christian	fundamentally
access	Christianity	length
accessible	coming	lengthening
accident	curiosity	speaking
accidental	curious	strength
accidentally	decided	you're
across	decision	
article	disciple	

In this chapter and in the three which follow you will learn how to master certain fundamental rules of spelling. Memorizing the spelling of a word is of course better than memorizing the "rule" for spelling. But rules do explain how certain groups of commonly misspelled words should be spelled. Exceptions to almost every rule do occur. When they do occur, you must learn them. Nevertheless, if you master the few rules—and the words which illustrate them—you should be able to conquer most of your spelling difficulties.

APOSTROPHES

The apostrophe is *a mark of omission:* it indicates that a word has been contracted; that a letter or letters which belong to it have been intentionally left out. Serious errors in spelling result from confusion about the various functions of the apostrophe. To reduce the number of errors study carefully each of the uses considered below.

CONTRACTION

The simplest and least troublesome function of the apostrophe is to show contraction—the omission from a word of one or more letters. In the examples of typical contractions shown here, note that the *apostrophe appears precisely where the original letter has been omitted.*

I am	contracts to	I'm
you are		you're
he is		he's
she is		she's
it is		it's
we are		we're
they are		they're

I you we they }	do not	don't
he she it }	does not	doesn't

I should have	I should've
I would have	I would've
I shall (or will)	I'll
I have	I've

NEVER USE **should of** / **would of**

I should not	I shouldn't
I would not	I wouldn't
who is	who's

POSSESSION

The chief problem in spelling with apostrophes results from confusing *contracted* forms with *possessive* forms. Where, for example, would you place or omit apostrophes in the following sentence?

Its its own food its eating.

Or, which words in parentheses would you use in the following sentence?

(Their, They're) bringing (their, they're) own lunch. (Who's, Whose) preparing (who's, whose) sandwiches in our home?

Solution:

1. *Think of contractions and possessives as entirely separate and distinct* in both **function and form:**

Function
Contractions use the apostrophe solely to indicate omission:

cannot becomes *can't*

Possessives generally use the apostrophe—and the letter *s*—to indicate ownership:

dog becomes *dog's* (as in *dog's* bone)

NOTE: **Personal and relative pronouns merely add the letter s; they do not use the apostrophe to show possession:**

it becomes *its* (as in Give the dog *its* bone.)

who becomes *whose* (as in I know *whose* book this is.)

Form
Contractions *link two words* to form a single word:

three *of the clock* becomes three *o'clock*

Possessives *begin and end as single words:*

her-hers; their-theirs; your-yours
John-John's; mother-mother's; cow-cow's

2. Try the problem word both ways—as contraction and as possessive. You will quickly see the distinction. For example, look again at the sentences above:

It is its own food it is eating—**This combination** makes sense. *It is* contracts meaningfully to *It's*

its (its own food) is a personal pronoun and requires an *s* but no apostrophe.

it is (eating) contracts meaningfully to *it's*.

They are (*They're*) bringing *their* own lunch.

Who is (*Who's*) preparing *whose* sandwiches in our home?

They're and *Who's* are contractions.

their and *whose* are possessive forms of the personal and relative pronoun respectively.

HINT: Steps 1 and 2 in solving the problem of apostrophes suggest both an attitude toward the problem and an experimental method of dealing with it. The remaining steps will clarify the principles behind these steps.

3. Learn the ways in which the apostrophe indicates possession.

Use apostrophes to show possession with:

Nouns

Singular nouns that do not end in *s* add an apostrophe and the letter *s*:

John's hat   Mary's book
cow's milk   company's books

Singular nouns that end in *s* add only the apostrophe:

Dickens' novels   Jones' estate
Keats' sonnets   hostess' gown

Plural nouns that do not end in *s* add an apostrophe and the letter *s*:

men's suits   people's voices
women's dresses   freshmen's foolishness
oxen's yokes   children's toys

Plural nouns that end in *s* add only the apostrophe:

writers' conference Negroes' rights
girls' clothes   boys' games
foxes' tails   monkeys' tricks
Joneses' estates   hostesses' gowns

Groups of words containing a single idea add an apostrophe and the letter *s* to the last word:

Art and Sofia's baby
John and May's automobile

Indefinite Pronouns

Such pronouns refer to persons or things generally rather than specifically.

anybody's guess   someone's radio
everybody's friend   everyone's taste
nobody's sweetheart

Exercise No. 25

Place the apostrophe, or the apostrophe and the letter *s*, wherever required.

1. gentlemens agreement
2. ten o clock
3. heros reception
4. theyre here
5. suns rays
6. youll see
7. Melissas doll
8. Twains novels
9. boys wear boys clothes
10. Achilles heel
11. Prince of Wales wife
12. Whos there?
13. yeomens chores
14. nobodys home in our house
15. nobodys house
16. Art and Libbys godchild
17. princesses gowns
18. Williams sermons
19. heres health
20. childrens pleasures

4. Learn when you should not use apostrophes to indicate possession.
   Never use apostrophes to show possession with *personal* or *relative* pronouns. These pronouns form their own possessive forms without the apostrophe.

Personal   *Relative*
his book   *Whose* house is that?
the hat is *hers*
its house
the notes are *ours*
the music is *theirs*

Never use apostrophes to form the possessive of nouns that stand for *inanimate objects*.

Write	**Not**
the call of the wild	the wild's call
the flowers of the meadow	the meadow's flowers
pages of a book	the book's pages
principles of logic	logic's principles
evils of money	money's evils

If, however, the expression is idiomatic, the possessive form may be used:

wit's end   moon's rays
duty's call   earth's surface
hair's breadth   razor's edge

5. Learn the Other Uses of the Apostrophe.
Use it to form the plurals of:
  Letters—four *e*'s; *Y.M.C.A.*'s; *x*'s and *y*'s.
  Numbers—1930's.
  Words referred to as words—How many *two*'s are there in that sentence?
Use it to represent colloquial speech:
  "Good *mornin'*," smiled the policeman. "Are you *goin'* to be *singin'* that tune all day?"

Exercise No. 26

This exercise reviews all the principles you have learned about the use of the apostrophe. Do not proceed to the section on *capitals* until you have mastered this exercise.

In the following paragraph: a. Place apostrophes where required. b. Select the appropriate word from the parentheses.

Shes the kind of woman who thinks that everybodys problems are hers. Well, we dont need her help. Other peoples notions apply to (their, they're) special needs: everybodys situation has its special quirk. Its time we regarded our problem as ours, not (anybody's, anybody) (else's, else). (Who's, Whose) solution wouldve been better well not know for many years, but at least ours will be yours and mine, not hers.

CAPITALS

Capitalization is a conventional device intended to ease the reader's way, but faulty capitalization impedes it. The initial capital signifies that a word is a proper noun or adjective (or to be considered as one), or that a new sentence or line of verse succeeds a former.

Use an initial capital letter:

To mark a proper noun or adjective, a title of distinction, a common noun personified, a reference to Deity.
Proper names: Andrew Jackson, Texas, England, Oxford
Proper adjectives: Jacksonian, Texan, English, Oxfordian
Races, ethnic groups, religions, (and the people who belong to them): Caucasian, Judaism, Catholicism, Negro, Jew, Protestant, Buddhist
Deity: God, Jehovah, Jove, Brahma, His word
Wars and Battles: World War II, Battle of the Bulge
Days and Months: Monday, October
Companies, organizations, clubs: Associated Press, General Motors Corporation, Young Men's Christian Association, Rotary
Geographical divisions: the Hudson River, the West, Pike's Peak, the North Pole, the East Side, Fifth Avenue, Piccadilly, Main Street
Official bodies: the United States Senate and House of Representatives
Titles of distinction: Bishop of New York, Duke of York, Superintendent of Documents
Personifications: There, Honor battled Ease. The Chair recognizes nobody
Specific courses: Economics 10, Mathematics 21

To mark the first word of every sentence, line of verse, and full quotation.

A man must eat.

Hope springs eternal in the human breast:
Man never is, but always to be blest. (Pope)

"In a republic," wrote Calvin Coolidge, "the law reflects rather than makes the standard of conduct and the state of popular opinion."

To mark the pronoun *I* and the interjection *O*.

It was I.

Who could have thought such starkness lay concealed
Within thy beams, O Sun! (Blanco White)

To mark a word signifying family relationship when used as a name.

Yes, Father said he would.
(But: My father said he would.)

Do not use the initial capital letter:
To mark general or class names.

Every boy wants to be president.
President Eisenhower was once a five-star general.

Though he was a democrat in principle, he did not belong to the Democratic Party.

To mark a point of the compass, save where it refers to a recognized geographical division.

Lars Porsena sent his men north, south, east, and west.
(But: The South has become an industrial area.)

To mark the seasons of the year.
spring, summer, autumn, fall

Exercise No. 27

Use an initial capital letter for the words requiring capitalization.

1. the anglo-saxon language was the language of our saxon forefathers in england, though they never gave it that name. they called it english. thus king alfred speaks of translating "from book-latin into english"; abbot aelfric was requested by aethelward "to translate the book of genesis from latin into english"; and bishop leofric, speaking of the manuscript (the "exeter manuscript") he gave to exeter cathedral, calls it "a great english book."

2. the city of nome, alaska, acquired its name through error. there was a small prospectors' settlement known as anvil city on the seward peninsula in alaska. a washington clerk, in drawing a map, did not know its name, and wrote "name?" at that place on the map. one of his superiors took the word for "nome" and that name still stands.

3. *stories in the modern manner*, edited by philip rahv and william phillips, was published by avon books. perhaps the best story in it is gide's "theseus."

4. the lion is a kingly beast.
   he likes a hindu for a feast.

5. it is the grace of god that urges missionaries to suffer the most disheartening privations for the faith. this grace moved saint isaac jogues to say (when he came to canada), "i felt as if it were a christmas day for me, and that i was to be born again to a new life, to a life in him."

Mastery Test Number 7

Do not proceed to the next chapter until you have taken this test. Master the spelling of these words from the *core list* before you try to learn those in the chapters ahead. Remember: in spelling your goal is a perfect score.

I. Add the appropriate suffix to complete the core list word.

EXAMPLE: This food is indigest.... (-able, -ible). indiges*tible*.

1. Academic.... (ly, aly, ally) speaking, he is not doing very good work.
2. The roadway has been repaired and is now access.... (able, ible).

3. The nominee made his accept....
(ence, ance) speech before a happy
audience.

4. The boy's request for an increase in
allowance was accept.... (ible, able)
to his parents.

5. Is the presence of a fly in my soup
really accident.... (al, el)?

6. Did the soldier shoot himself in the
foot accident.... (ly, elly, ally) or
purposely?

7. I am basic.... (ly, ally, illy) in ac-
cord with your views.

8. We have final.... (y, ly) arrived at
our point of embarkation.

9. There can be no fundament.... (il,
al, el) distinction between identical
twins.

10. Although details need to be clarified,
his essay is fundament.... (ly, ally,
elly) sound.

II. One word in each of the following groups
is correctly spelled. Choose the word.

1. After much deliberation, the jury
reached a (descision, decision, de-
sision).

2. Many great writers belong to the
American (Aocademy, Acaddemy,
Academy) of Arts and Letters.

3. I have been granted (axcess, accss,
access) to the department's secret
files.

4. The dominant religion in Western
Europe is (Chirstianity, Cristianity,
Christianity).

5. The *Encyclopaedia* (*Brittanica, Britannica, Brittannica*) is one of the most
important reference books in the
world.

6. The automobile (acident, accident,
aciddent) cost two men their lives.

7. Look (across, accross, accros) the
field.

8. I shall (challenge, chalenge, chal-
lange) him to a duel.

9. She has a searching and relentless
(curosity, curriosity, curiosity) about
the nature of things.

10. A wayward child needs gentle but firm
(dissipline, discipline, disipline).

III. One of the core list words in each of the
following sentences contains an extra letter that causes a misspelling. Remove the
extra letter.

1. I remember when Brittain really ruled
the waves.

2. The quarterback's acaddemic record
was not spectacularly good.

3. Androcles was a Roman by birth, a
Christtian by faith.

4. Lenghthening or shortening hemlines
seems to be the major activity of the
contemporary fashion designer.

5. I can find no logical bassis for lower-
ing standards for admission to college.

6. Whom did you meet while comming
through the rye?

7. Familliar faces need not always be
welcome sights.

8. I am currious to learn how one so dull
became so successful.

9. Every leader has a band of discipeles
who follow him slavishly.

10. I acceppt your terms unconditionally.

IV. Proofread the following passage, correcting all errors in spelling.

I have decidid that your artecle does'nt
have enough strenth of conviction. Before
acepting it, I should like you to increase
its lenkth, strenthen its style, and support
its arguments more forcefully. When, for
example, your'e speaking of Chirst, Bud-

dha, Lao-Tse, ect., you need to draw clearer distinctions among them.

SPECIAL WORD SECTION— LITERATURE

The following words appear frequently in literary works, reviews of literary works, and in books. Often they are misspelled. Master their spelling; then test your knowledge of their *spelling* and *meaning* in the exercise that follows.

autobiography	novel
bibliography	picaresque
classicism	prologue
comedy	realism
drama	rhyme
essay	rhythm
imagery	romanticism
lyric	satire
meter (metre)	soliloquy
narrative	tragedy

Special Word Exercise No. 7

Complete the following sentences by choosing the appropriate word from the list below. *If any word in the list is incorrectly spelled, correct it.*

I.

1. While the aging statesman writes his ......, eager biographers impatiently await his death.
2. Our decade continues to prefer the narrative form of the ...... to the expository form of the ....
3. In ......, characters come to a happy end; in ...... to an unhappy one.

essey   novil   autobiography
tradegy   comedy

II.

1. ......, by portraying the actual and typical, reacted against the invention and imaginative excess of ......
2. ......, closer to realism than to romanticism, often reveals a bias toward pessimism.
3. Reason, restraint, simplicity, and balance are central to the great writings of ....
4. To wound, to ridicule, to parody—these are some of the purposes of ....

sattire   reelism   romanticism
naturelism   classisim

III.

1. Before one prepares a ...... of English ......, he should list the names of innumerable playwrights whose works are to be included.
2. In the ...... novel, the roguish hero wanders abroad so frequently that the ...... seems to have no central thread.
3. To give a ......, an actor must assume that no one is listening to him as he speaks aloud his private thoughts.

drama   narattive   piceresque
bibliography   sololoquy

IV.

1. As a poem the ...... represents an outburst of emotion rather than a narrative.
2. Metaphor and simile are the most conventional figures of poetic ....
3. Before the curtain rose the actor recited the ...... Its lines were swift in ..... but they did not ....

imagry, ryhthm, ryhme,
liric, prologue

CHAPTER NINE

LEARNING THE RULES: IE AND EI

CORE LIST

atheist	field	liveliest
attendance	financially	livelihood
attendant	financier	liveliness
attended	friend	lives
author	friendliness	ninety
authoritative	gaiety	perceive
authority	happiness	piece
before	influence	relieve
careful	influential	seize
careless	involve	view
chief	knowledge	weird
deceive	laboratory	yield
dependent	leisure	
entertain	leisurely	

Use i before e, when sounded as ee,
Except after c,
Or when sounded like a,
As in neighbor and weigh.

You need not despair if the time-worn jingle about ie and ei has not always rewarded you with the final clue to spelling accuracy. The jingle is the key that opens for you a vault containing innumerable words. All you need are a few extra keys for some smaller locked chests in that vault.

However, before you unlock the word hoards in those small chests, learn how to use the "jingle key" that opens the central treasury:

Use i before e when ie is pronounced ee (as in week or meek)—except after c. Study the typical examples given:

IE Pronounced As EE

achieve	field	reprieve
apiece	fiend	shield
belief	fierce	shriek
believe	frieze	siege
bier	grief	thief
brief	niece	tier
cashier	piece	wield
chief	pierce	yield

After the letter c, use e before i, even though the pronunciation is ee. Study the typical examples given:

ceiling	deceit
perceive	deceive
conceit	receive
conceive	receipt

The principles illustrated above derive from the first two lines of the jingle. Now learn the words based upon the second couplet:

Use e before i when ei is pronounced as a (as in neighbor and weigh). Study the typical examples given:

feint	reign	weight
freight	skein	veil
rein	heinous	feign
deign	eighth	inveigh
neigh	sleigh	vein

Exercise No. 28

Do not proceed until your score on this exercise is perfect.

Complete the spelling of the following words by filling in **ie** or **ei** in the blank spaces.

1. h..nous crime
2. cash..r's check
3. inv..gh against sin
4. d..gn to reply
5. foul f..nd
6. b..r of the deceased
7. w..ld a knife
8. t..r of seats
9. sl..gh ride
10. f..gn surprise
11. sk..n of wool
12. last minute repr..ve
13. f..rce savage
14. y..ld to force
15. ach..ve success

If you have attained a perfect score on this exercise, you are prepared to open those "smaller chests" of words mentioned earlier. Use one key at a time; avoid trying to open all the chests at once. In brief, study one item and master it before proceeding to the next.

Extra Keys to the IE Word Hoard

1. Use **ie** after a sh sound—even after **c**.

   sufficient: fic is pronounced **fish**. After **sh** sound, use **ie**.

   HINT: In words of this kind, the **ie** occurs in an unaccented syllable where it is pronounced as **eh** or **uh** rather than **ee**.

   Study the examples given:

ancient	deficient	proficient
quotient	species	transient
patient	conscience	omniscience

2. Use **ie** to spell **friend**—the only occasion on which **ie** is sounded as **e** in **end** (end in friend).

Extra Keys to the EI Word Hoard

1. Use **ei** if sounded as short **i** (as in **hit**):

counterfeit	heifer
foreign	surfeit
sovereign	forfeit

   But note these exceptions: sieve, mischief, mischievous, handkerchief.

2. Use **ei** if sounded as long **i** (as in **ice**):

eider	height	sleight
stein	heigh-ho	kaleidoscope
		seismograph

3. Use **ei** in the following words with long **ee** sounds. Originally, these words were pronounced a (*neighbor*), i (*hit*), or i (*ice*), and thus were spelled consistent with their pronunciations. But American pronunciation—*ee* as in *meet*—makes them seem to be exceptions to the rules.

either	neither
weird	seize
weir	inveigle
leisure	sheik

4. Note this single exception to all **ei** rules: financier

An Extra Key to the IE-EI Word Hoard

If **i** and **e** do not form a *digraph* (two letters used to represent a single sound), the principles hitherto discussed do not apply. You must therefore attend carefully to the pronunciation of each word.

fiery breaks into **fi ery**. Since the **i** and **e** have independent sound values, they cannot be considered a digraph. The same principle applies to the words listed below:

clothier   glacier
hygiene   science
sobriety   audience
gaiety   alien
medieval   quiet
society   notoriety
hierarchy   deity

HINT: Although no rule applies to these words, all of them except **deity** are spelled with **ie**.

Exercise No. 29

Review Test of IE and EI

Do not proceed to the Mastery Test until you have a perfect score on this Review Test. Many of these words will reappear on the Mastery Test for this chapter. Make certain of your spelling strength before you go on.

Complete the following words by filling in **ie** or **ei** in the blank spaces.

1. gr..f-stricken
2. pagan d..ty
3. cow's h..fer
4. human spec..s
5. w..rd mask
6. intelligence quot..nt
7. frozen glac..r
8. guilty consc..nce
9. unbridled ga..ty
10. ..ther or n..ther
11. trans..nt hotel
12. for..gn agent
13. inv..gled dupe
14. signed rec..pt
15. v..n of iron
16. w..ld power
17. shr..k with rage
18. v..led reference
19. s..zure of land
20. good n..ghbor

21. horse r..ns
22. sleek sh..k
23. pat..nt Griselda
24. silent sobr..ty
25. rel..f rolls
26. pr..stly h..rarchy
27. profic..nt student
28. ..der down
29. vitamin defic..ncy
30. counterf..t money
31. sover..gn lord
32. l..sure time
33. dec..tful lie
34. al..n quota
35. med..val history
36. surf..ted appetite
37. anc..nt mariner
38. qu..t man
39. misch..f-maker
40. ch..f miner
41. perc..ve differences
42. br..f encounter
43. c..ling zero
44. f..ld of clover
45. p..r boss
46. f..ry furnace
47. best fr..nd
48. omnisc..nt genius
49. solemn m..n
50. wealthy financ..r

Mastery Test Number 8

Do not proceed to the next chapter until you have taken this test. Master the spelling of these words from the **core list** before you try to learn those in the chapters ahead. Remember: in spelling your goal is a perfect score.

I. Insert *ie* or *ei* in the blank spaces.

1. Is the dog man's best fr..nd?
2. Can you name the three w..rd sisters in *Macbeth?*

3. The ath..st denies the existence of God.
4. What is your ch..f reason for refusing to attend the lecture?
5. Woman, arch dec..ver of mankind.
6. I should like to lie in a f..ld of clover.
7. Pierpont Morgan was one of Wall Street's greatest financ..rs.
8. New Orleans' Mardi Gras is famed for its sprightly ga..ty.
9. This summer I plan to relax and make full use of my l..sure.
10. I cannot perc..ve the difference between the two texts.
11. The policeman tried to s..ze the fleeing robber.
12. I want a room with a v..w of the bay.
13. I will not y..ld to pressure.
14. May I have another p..ce of cake?
15. Aspirin may rel..ve your headache.

II. Each of the core list words in the following sentences either A. *Needs an extra letter;* B. *Has an extra letter.* In either case correct the spelling.

1. Financialy, I am in dire straits. More simply, I'm broke.
2. I intend to drive across the nation leisurly, stopping every few hours for a rest.
3. The courtroom atendant brought the prisoner before the bar.
4. I am seeking a definitive, authorittative opinion that will settle the problem.
5. We look befor and after and sigh for what is not.
6. Carless people make costly mistakes.
7. I have no knowlege of physics.
8. Once I worked in a chemical labratory as a testtube cleaner.
9. I have in my day earned a livlihood as a dishwasher.

10. The car sped along at ninnety miles per hour.
11. What authorrity have you to enter my apartment without my permission?
12. Be carefull what you say about my mother-in-law.
13. Everyone wants a little hapiness in his life.
14. If you know an inffluential man, you may be able to get an apartment without waiting.
15. Livliness and wit may effectively replace physical beauty.

III. Proofread the following passage, correcting all errors in spelling.

The authurs freindliness entertained those in attendence at the lecture. Had their lifes been as involved as those of his fictional characters, however (none of whom would have atended lectures of any kind), even his livliest manner would have failed to influance them, for they seemed to be dependant solely upon a sense of personal misery and failure.

SPECIAL WORD SECTION— PSYCHOLOGY

The words listed below appear frequently in popular articles about psychology and in books. Often they are misspelled. Master their spelling; then test your knowledge of their *spelling* and *meaning* in the exercise that follows.

amnesia	paranoid
anxiety	psychiatry
aptitude	psychoanalysis
claustrophobia	psychosis
empirical	psychosomatic
hysteria	rapport
inhibition	repression
intelligence	senility
neurosis	sublimation
Oedipus complex	transference

Special Word Exercise No. 8

Complete the following sentences by choosing the appropriate word from the list below. *If the word in the list is incorrectly spelled, correct it.*

I.

1. Fear, apprehension, and foreboding afflict one suffering from . . . .
2. In . . . . . ., Freud's method of treating personality disorders is more rigid than that employed in . . . .
3. A patient suffering from an . . . . . . may, at the stage of therapy known as . . . . . ., shift his feelings of hostility from a parent to his analyst.

  Odepuss complex, pshychoanalysis, psychiatry, transferance, anxiety

II.

1. Prolonged . . . . . . of conscious impulses and desires may on occasion erupt in an acute nervous disorder known as . . . . . .
2. The victim of . . . . . . fears enclosed spaces; the victim of . . . . . . forgets who he is.
3. The young need not fear . . . . . .; even the old, if they remain young in heart, need not fear it.

  amnisia, repression, clauserophobia, hystaria, senility

III.

1. Indigestion, ulcers, and related ailments may often be . . . . . . in origin, the body manifesting the disturbance in the mind.
2. . . . . . . personalities suffer from delusions of persecution, grandeur, and the like.
3. A certain number of . . . . . . can profitably be tolerated by any person, but too many frustrated desires may cause trouble.
4. A mild mental disturbance is a . . . . . .; a severe one a . . . .

  paranoid, psychosis, nurosis, inhibisions, pshychosometic

IV.

1. Psychology, an . . . . . . science, bases its conclusions on observation and experiment.
2. Tests designed to predict vocational skills are known as . . . . . . tests; those designed to measure a stage of mental development are known as . . . . . . tests.
3. By . . . . . ., the analyst seeks to redirect antisocial urges into socially acceptable ones.
4. Analysts strive to achieve . . . . . . with their patients, a sense of common interest and feeling that makes the patient trust his analyst.

  sublimeation, inteligence, aptitude, empirical, rapaport

CHAPTER TEN

PASS YOUR FINALS: FINAL SILENT E; FINAL Y; FINAL CONSONANTS

CORE LIST

accompanied	changeable	stories
accompanies	changing	story
accompaniment	companies	sufficient
accompanying	company	swimming
advantage	connotation	theories
advantageous	connote	theory
applies	council	transferred
applying	counsel	omit
buried	counselor	omitted
bury	countries	parallel
carried	desirability	particular
carrier	desire	permit
carries	extremely	
carrying	sincerely	

The three rules grouped in this chapter share a single likeness: they enable you to avoid spelling errors common at the *end of words*. When you master these few rules, you should unfailingly spell correctly words like:

Final silent e:	lovable	(not loveable)
	peaceable	(not peacable)
Final y:	flies	(not flys)
	copies	(not copys)
Final consonants:	conferring	(not confering)
	shining	(not shinning)

Study each rule carefully. Master it and its illustrative words before proceeding to the next rule.

FINAL SILENT E

Final silent e causes difficulty because it is sometimes *dropped* before a suffix and sometimes *retained*. Two rules will help you solve most of the difficulties.

1. **Drop final silent e before a suffix beginning with a vowel.**
   grieve drops final silent e before suffix—
   -ance which begins with vowel **a**.
   Therefore—**grievance**

Study the following examples:

argue	arguing
become	becoming
bare	baring
change	changing
force	forcible
conceive	conceivable
hope	hoping
come	coming
admire	admirable
desire	desirable
have	having
judge	judging
dine	dining
mistake	mistakable
move	movable

pursue — pursuing
sale — salable
use — using, usable, usage
write — writing
value — valuable

2. **Retain** final silent **e** before a **suffix** beginning with a **consonant.**

achieve retains final silent **e** before suffix — -ment which begins with consonant **m.**

Therefore—**achievement**

Study the following examples:

absolute — absolutely
arrange — arrangement
care — careless
complete — completely
definite — definitely
hope — hopeless
like — likelihood, likely
live — lively, liveliness
lone — lonely, loneliness
love — lovely, loveliness
nine — ninety, nineteen
sure — surely

Exercise No. 30

Complete the spelling of the following words by filling in *e* where necessary. If no *e* is needed, leave the space blank.

1. us..able tools
2. din..ing car
3. mov..able furniture
4. hav..ing wonderful time
5. conceiv..able notion
6. lik..lihood
7. admir..able butler
8. sur..ly
9. lik..able lad
10. car..less love
11. sal..able products
12. com..ing home
13. lon..liness
14. mistak..able notion
15. desir..able girl

Although the rules you have just learned do not, unfortunately, apply to all words with final silent e, the exceptions can be easily grouped and learned.

1. **Drop** final silent **e** after the letters **u** or **w.**

true ly — becomes **truly**
awe ful — becomes **awful**
due ly — becomes **duly**
argue ment — becomes **argument**

2. **Retain** final silent **e** after **soft c** (as in **fancy**) or **soft g** (as in **range**) before suffixes beginning with **a** or **o.**

peaceable—Retaining the **e** keeps the **c** soft. Otherwise, the word would be *peacable* (to rhyme with *peekable*).

changeable—Retaining the **e** keeps the **g** soft. Otherwise, the word would be *changable* (to rhyme with *hangable*).

Study the following examples:

advantage — advantageous
change — changeable
courage — courageous
service — serviceable
notice — noticeable
outrage — outrageous
manage — manageable
trace — traceable

3. **Retain** final silent **e** before the suffix **-ing** to avoid mispronunciation or ambiguity.

singe ("to scorch")—singeing
but sing ("to chant")—singing
dye ("to color")—dyeing
but die ("to cease to live")—dying

4. Retain final silent **e** when the endings -ye, -oe, -ee precede the suffix -ing.

eye—eyeing
hoe—hoeing
shoe—shoeing
decree—decreeing
see—seeing
agree—agreeing
guarantee—guaranteeing
toe—toeing

Exercise No. 31

Review test on Final Silent e.

Do not proceed to the next rule until you achieve a perfect score on this test.

Complete the spelling of the following words by filling in *e* where necessary. If no *e* is needed, leave the space blank.

1. dy..ing her hair
2. judg..ing horses
3. to..ing the line
4. du..ly argu..d
5. lov..ly day
6. sing..ing hair
7. sing..ing loud
8. advantag..ous spot
9. not agre..ing
10. pursu..ing rainbows
11. courag..ous man
12. desir..able girl
13. chang..able mood
14. tru..ly yours
15. sho..ing the horse
16. dy..ing of boredom
17. outrag..ous behavior
18. servic..able machine
19. swing..ing a horse
20. good us..age

FINAL Y

Two rules will help you to solve most of the problem endings that followed final *y*.

1. **Retain** final y if it is preceded by a **vowel.**

Nouns Singular	Plural (retain final y; add s)
attorney	attorneys
boy	boys
day	days
joy	joys
key	keys
play	plays
trolley	trolleys
turkey	turkeys
valley	valleys
journey	journeys
chimney	chimneys

Verbs	Present (3rd Person Singular)
relay	relays
stay	stays
play	plays
enjoy	enjoys
employ	employs

Past	Present Participle
relayed	relaying
stayed	staying
played	playing
enjoyed	enjoying
employed	employing

HINT: Learn these exceptions:

day—daily	pay—paid	lay—laid
say—said	slay—slain	

2. **Change** final y to **i** if it is preceded by a **consonant.**

Nouns	Singular	Plural (change y to i and add -es)
	army	armies
	baby	babies
	beauty	beauties
	copy	copies
	company	companies
	cry	cries
	country	countries
	family	families
	lady	ladies
	sky	skies

Singular Verbs	Present (3rd Person Singular)	Past	Present Participle
bury	buries	buried	burying
deny	denies	denied	denying
hurry	hurries	hurried	hurrying
marry	marries	married	marrying
ply	plies	plied	plying
rely	relies	relied	relying
reply	replies	replied	replying
satisfy	satisfies	satisfied	satisfying
study	studies	studied	studying
try	tries	tried	trying

Exercise No. 32

Complete the spelling of the following words by filling in the blank space with *y* or *i* (or *ie*).

1. trolle..s
2. famil..s
3. emplo..s
4. valle..s
5. cop..s
6. sla..n
7. pl..d
8. cr..s
9. pla..ed
10. marr..ing
11. hurr..ing
12. satisf..d
13. turke..s
14. marr..d
15. da..ly
16. rel..s
17. journe..s
18. enjo..s
19. ke..s
20. bur..s

The following observations will help you to master many of the exceptions to the rules given above.

1. **Change final y to i when preceded by a consonant and followed by a suffix—except when the suffix begins with i.**

beauty	beautiful	lonely	loneliness
busy	business	marry	marriage
carry	carriage	mercy	merciful
easy	easily	mystery	mysterious
envy	envious	study	studious

But, when the suffix begins with **i**: carrying, occupying, trying, playing, and the like

2. Retain final y before certain suffixes.

employment	shyness	dryness	playful
enjoyment	coyness	slyness	joyful

FINAL CONSONANTS

Failure to know when to double a final consonant produces amusing but damaging results:

> He was *filing* (for **filling**) his glass with wine.
> *Moby Dick* is a *griping* (for **gripping**) novel.
> The cleaning women did their *moping* (for **mopping**) every evening.

The rules for doubling may at first seem complicated. Actually they are not. Learn each step as it is presented—rule and application. Your efforts will be rewarded when you confront with assurance innumerable words to which these rules apply.

Double a final single consonant when:
> It is preceded by a single vowel (b**a**t)
> It is followed by a suffix beginning with a vowel (sit **t** ing)
> It appears in a monosyllabic (one syllable) word (**hit, run**)
>
> **or**
>
> It appears in a word accented on the last syllable (o **mit'**)

Study the rule at work in the following examples:

1. stop—**stopped, stopping**
   Final consonant **p** is preceded by single vowel **o**
   Final consonant **p** is followed by suffix (**-ed, -ing**) beginning with a vowel
   stop is a monosyllabic word
2. occur—**occurred, occurring, occurrence**
   Final consonant **r** is preceded by a single vowel **u**

Final consonant **r** is followed by suffix (**-ed, -ing, -ence**) beginning with a vowel. **oc cur'** is accented on the second syllable.
Study the following list of monosyllabic and polysyllabic words whose final consonants are doubled:

Monosyllables		*Polysyllables*	
beg	man	acquit	omit
brag	plan	allot	permit
cram	quit	begin	prefer
drop	ship	commit	submit
get	stab	forbid	run
rob	whip	refer	transfer

Do not double a final single consonant when:
The accent is shifted to a preceding syllable when the suffix is added.

> confer'—confer' r ing **but con' ference**
> refer'—refer' r ed **but re' ference**

Conferring and **referred** fulfil the rules for doubling the final consonant.

But *con'ference* and *re'ference* shift their accents to the first syllable, and so do not apply to the rule that the accent must be on the first syllable.
Study the following list of words whose final consonant does not double:

preference	benefited
counseled	conquerable
happened	marveled
traveled	kidnaped
inference	deference

Exercise No. 33

Review Test on Final silent e, final y, and final consonants.

Do not proceed to the Mastery Test for this chapter until you have attained a perfect score on this review test.

Complete the spelling of the following words by filling in the blanks where necessary. If the word is correct, leave it as is.

1. win..ing smile
2. stud..ing hard
3. boil..ing mad
4. dr..ness in the air
5. quit..ing work
6. forbid..ing look
7. com..ing home
8. marvel..ous boy
9. travel..ed far
10. myster..ous woman
11. bus..ness man
12. chang..able manners
13. man tr..s his best
14. hungry bab..s
15. da..ly bread
16. whip..ing post
17. commit..ed murder
18. no prefer..ence
19. fast run..er
20. victim was stab..ed
21. fil..ing his stomach
22. unmistak..ably wrong
23. loud brag..ing
24. sk..s of blue
25. eerie cr..s
26. notic..able gap
27. crack in the c..ling
28. stop..ing for lunch
29. happy occur..ence
30. refer..ence book
31. writ..ing assignment
32. grip..ing novel
33. inconquer..able soul
34. affected co..ness
35. happy marr..age
36. env..ous girl
37. pl..s his trade
38. lost his ke..s
39. fighting arm..s
40. la.. the book down yesterday
41. la.. down for a rest yesterday
42. had l.. the book down
43. has l.. down for a rest
44. wisely counsel..ed
45. den..d the charges
46. baby sit..ing
47. omit..ed pages
48. begin..er's luck
49. gifts for lad..s
50. man..ish appearance

Mastery Test Number 9

Do not proceed to the next chapter until you have taken this test. Master the spelling of these words from the **core list** before you try to learn those in the chapters ahead. Remember: in spelling your goal is a perfect score.

I. In each of the italicized words in the following sentences, a blank space has been left for *one* letter. Add the appropriate letter.

1. Will Joe be *carr..ing* your books this afternoon?
2. Send the water *carr..er* on to the field.
3. I question the *desir..bility* of visiting him at this time.
4. He has been *extrem..ly* ill for several weeks.
5. The countess was *accompan..ed* by her husband.
6. It is always *advantag..ous* to buy two books for the price of one.
7. What I say to your brother *appl..es* to you as well.
8. He is a man of extremely *chang..able* moods.
9. How many *compan..es* went into bankruptcy last year?
10. I have been counting the number of *countr..es* in western Europe.

II. Some of the italicized words in the following sentences require *single* consonants; some require *double* consonants. Fill the blank with the appropriate number of consonants.

> EXAMPLE: He is fi..ing the cup
> (consonant: l)   Answer—filling
>
> He is fi...ing his nails
> (consonant: l)   Answer—filing

1. You have *omi..ed* two questions from your answer paper. (t)
2. Will you go *swi..ing* with me this afternoon? (m)
3. The prospectors searched for the *bu..ied* gold. (r)
4. The policeman was *transfe..ed* to a new precinct. (r)
5. Two lines running exactly beside one another are called *para..e...* (l)
6. The word "Mom" *co..otes* a richer emotional tone than the word "Mother." (n)
7. Will your sister be *a..ompanying* you to the dance? (c)
8. The groom *ca..ied* his bride across the threshold. (r)
9. If I am called to trial I shall ask my *counse..or* to represent me. (l)
10. Two spoonfuls of sugar will be *su..icient* for my tea. (f)

III. One word in each of the following groups is correctly spelled. Choose the word.

1. Lobbyists are most (particlar, particular, partikular) about the congressmen they buttonhole.
2. Machinists are more effective with practical matters than they are with (theorys, theoreis, theories).
3. Numismatists recount exciting (stories, storys, storries) about the coins they have collected.
4. Optometrists listen to their patients' visual problems (sincerly, sincerely, sincerelly).
5. Politicians suffer from an inability to avoid words whose (conottation, connotation, conotation) arouses feeling rather than reflective thought.
6. Quail breeders are always watching to determine when their male stock needs (changeing, changing, changging).
7. Radio announcers spend their leisure time (appling, applieing, applying) for jobs in television.
8. Soloists in symphony orchestras rely upon intelligent (accompanyment, accompaniment, accompaniement) from their colleagues.
9. Tailors specialize in almost doing what their customers (dessire, dizire, desire).
10. Upholsterers often like to work in (commpany, company, comppany) with tack pullers.

IV. Proofread the following passage, correcting all errors in spelling.

Sometimes a newspaper editor will burry or ommit a storry—and the picture that accompanys it—that carrys references that do not show his favorite thoery to addvantage. Without avail a counsel of his fellow editors often council him not to permet his prejudice to corrupt his judgment.

SPECIAL WORD SECTION— ARCHITECTURE

The words listed below appear frequently in popular articles about architecture and in books. Often they are misspelled. Master their spelling; then test your knowledge of their *spelling* and *meaning* in the exercise that follows.

abutment girder
baroque   Gothic
buttress   lancet
Byzantine mosaic
cantilever nave
colonnade Romanesque
cornice   rotunda
corridor   trellis
façade   veneer
gargoyle wainscot

Special Word Exercise No. 9

Complete the following sentences by choosing the appropriate word from the list below. *If any word in the list is incorrectly spelled, correct it.*

I.

1. The ...... of a ...... building is usually flamboyant.
2. ...... cathedrals generally have towering spires, symbolic of man's spiritual aspirations.
3. The semi-darkness of a ...... abbey reflects the austerity of the monastic spirit.
4. Those fantastic animals projecting from building gutters are known as ....

barokue, Gothic, Romanesk,
gargoils, faceade

II.

1. Arch bridges are supported by ....

2. Skyscrapers use the ...... as their skeletal structure.
3. ...... windows allow light to fall upon the aisles and ...... of a cathedral.
4. The entrance hall of the Capitol in Washington, D.C. is known as a ....

lancet, knave, abuttments,
rotunder, girder

III.

1. ...... architecture is characterized by elaborate decoration.
2. The Parthenon in Greece has an exquisite arrangement of ...... around the outer portion of the building.
3. The walls of the church are supported by ...... which lean against it.
4. The floor of the entrance ...... to the mansion was made of inlaid ...... representing the birth of Venus.

moseaic, Byzanteen, colonades,
corridor, butteresses

IV.

1. The walls of the study were finished in ......, made of thin, mahogany ....
2. The vines grew wild on the cross strips of the garden ....
3. The ...... was elaborately decorated with wreaths and garlands; the rest of the wall was plain.
4. Terraces and bridges can both be supported by ...... beams.

trellus, venear, wainscott,
cornise, cantilever

CHAPTER ELEVEN

LEARNING THE RULES: "SEED" WORDS; *K*; *AI* AND *IA*

CORE LIST

accomplish	allowed	significance
accuracy	allows	speech
accurate	altar	sponsor
accurately	amateur	stabilization
admission	concede	susceptible
admit	continuous	those
admittance	paid	thought
afraid	physical	tomorrow
against	planned	tremendous
aggravate	pleasant	undoubtedly
alleviate	possible	vengeance
allotment	quantity	warrant
allotted	religion	
allow	response	

This chapter, though perhaps the shortest and simplest in the book, is one of the most valuable. In it you will learn some easy rules that should enable you to master some of the most frequently misspelled words in English.

"SEED" WORDS

The English language possesses only *twelve* words ending in the pronunciation "seed." All of these words (derived from the Latin root ced [cedere, "to yield"]) cause considerable spelling difficulty. The solution is extraordinarily simple.

1. Learn to spell these four words

    supersede
—the only word in English that ends in -sede.

exceed
proceed
succeed
—these three are the only words in English that end in -ceed.

2. Learn the remaining eight words—all of them in -cede.

accede	intercede
antecede	precede
cede	recede
concede	secede

Now that you have mastered the spelling of these words, you should:

1. Understand their meaning. Words like **supersede, exceed, accede, intercede** and **antecede** belong in your writing and speaking vocabulary. Do you use them?

2. Recognize their relationship to words derived from them.

proceed	—	pro*cede*ure, process
exceed	—	excessive
succeed	—	successive, succession
antecede	—	antecedent
accede	—	accession
concede	—	concession
recede	—	recessive, recession
secede	—	secession

K

Words ending in c often create spelling hazards. Avoid such errors by:
Adding k before a suffix beginning with e, i, or y. By so doing, you preserve the necessary hard *c* sound.

frolic	frolicked	frolicking
mimic	mimicked	mimicking
panic	panicked	panicking
picnic	picnicked	picnicking
traffic	trafficked	trafficking

AI AND IA

Deciding between **villain** and *villian* wastes time. Learn and apply these simple rules that save time and eliminate errors.

1. When **a** and **i** form a **digraph** (single sound) pronounced **eh** or **uh**, a comes before i.

villain	chieftain
captain	Britain
certain	mountain

2. When **i** and **a** are pronounced separately, or when they form a **yuh** sound, i comes before a.

Pronounced Separately	*Pronounced as yuh*
median (med **ee** an)	civilian (civil **yun**)
guardian	peculiar
genial	familiar
	auxiliary
	brilliant
	Christian
	genial

HINT: When these letters appear after c or t, place i before a to preserve the sh sound.

| beneficial | partial |
| financial | martial |

Exercise No. 34

Underline the one correctly spelled word in each of the following groups.

1. a. civilain b. civilian c. civillian
2. a. succeed b. sucede c. succede
3. a. supercede b. superceed c. supersede
4. a. benefficial b. beneficail c. beneficial
5. a. Christian b. Christain c. Christtain
6. a. intersede b. interseed c. intercede
7. a. antecedent b. anteceedent c. antesedent
8. a. proceedure b. procedure c. procedeure
9. a picnicing b. picniccing c. picnicking
10. a. exceed b. excede c. exsede
11. a. chieftian b. chieftain c. chiefftain
12. a. genial b. genail c. gennial
13. a. villein b. villian c. villain
14. a. Britain b. Britian c. Brittin
15. a. frolicing b. frolicking c. froliking
16. a. prosede b. procede c. proceed
17. a. succession b. sucession c. succesion
18. a. preceed b. precede c. presede
19. a. mimicry b. mimickry c. mimikry
20. a. auxilairy b. auxiliary c. auxilliary

Exercise No. 35

Review Test of Rules from Chapters Eight through Eleven.

Do not proceed to Chapter Twelve until you have achieved a perfect score on this review test. If you are uncertain about the rule underlying the spelling of any word, the answer key will refer you to the appropriate chapter. Do not, however, refer to the answer key until you have completed the entire test.

Apply the appropriate rule to the spelling of the following words. Thus, if apostrophes or capitals are lacking, supply them; if letters are missing, insert the proper letter or letters. If words are correctly written, let them alone.

1. Hildas French book
2. judaism

3. din..ing out
4. mathematics
5. joneses pools
6. youll be there
7. shouldve called
8. negros talents
9. d..ed hair
10. loser conc..s
11. nome, alaska
12. Maxs taxes
13. picni..ing
14. v..n of ore
15. la.. to rest
16. ex..d expectations
17. civil..n duties
18. reckless vill..n
19. tall mount..n
20. ill-conc..ved
21. four *ys*
22. people panic..ed
23. record is hers
24. history 108
25. rent c..ling
26. profic..nt student
27. father is home
28. english
29. tru..ly sorry
30. razors edge
31. theyd know
32. peace..able man
33. mondays child
34. pat..nt man
35. outrag..s behavior
36. l..sure moments
37. dickens stories
38. ruined financ..r
39. its cold
40. house is theirs
41. whose book
42. guard..ns angel
43. its hat
44. ten o clock
45. rich y..ld

46. youre crazy
47. mart..l pomp
48. heres mud in your eye
49. auxil..ry power
50. christ..n martyr

Mastery Test Number 10

Do not proceed to the next chapter until you have taken this test. Master the spelling of these words from the *core list* before you try to learn those in the chapters ahead. Remember: in spelling your goal is a perfect score.

I. Match the core list word with the appropriate context. If the core list word is misspelled, correct it.

Column A	*Column B*
1. This will relieve the pain	a. conseed
2. We strive to avoid price fluctuation	b. sponser
3. I yield to your argument	c. acurate
4. He wants his share	d. aggrevate
5. Your facts are entirely right	e. aleviate
6. He has no professional status	f. amatoor
7. Will he underwrite our venture?	g. stabilisation
8. He is disposed toward illness	h. suseptible
9. Don't make it worse	i. significence
10. What meaning does that sentence have?	j. allottment

II. One word in each of the following sentences is correctly spelled. Choose the word.

1. The rain on the plain in Spain last year was (continnuous, continuous, continueous).
2. We hope at last to be (payed, payd, paid) on time.

3. The army asked each man to submit to a (physical, pysical, phisical) examination.
4. You will (undoutedly, undoubtedly, undoubttedly) pass your intelligence tests.
5. (Acuracy, Accuraccy, Accuracy) in spelling is prerequisite to success in business.
6. I tried without success to gain (admittance, admitance, admittence) to the ball.
7. How much rice has been (alotted, alloted, allotted) to the needy people of Korea?
8. (Tommorrow, Tomorrow, Tommorow) creeps in this petty pace from day to day.
9. A heavyweight boxer has a (tremendous, tremenjus, tremenus) weight advantage over a flyweight.
10. The police issued a (warrent, warant, warrant) for the arrest of the escaped arsonist.

III. Each of the core list words in the following sentences either A. *Needs an extra letter*; B. *Has an extra letter*. In either case correct the spelling.

1. Abigail has already planed her summer vacation.
2. Beulah has a pleassant face but an irritating personality.
3. Cynthia always takes the path of least posible resistance.
4. Deborah has a huge quanity of war cries at her disposal.
5. Edith can acomplish any task she undertakes.
6. Frances charges addmission to all her parties.
7. Gertrude has always been affraid of lightning.

8. Hilda was alowed to carry a reduced program at college.
9. Irma has always been faithful to her relligion.
10. Judy invariably makes a ressponse to any comment she hears.

IV. Proofread the following passage, correcting all errors in spelling.

The minister left the alter for the pulpit. Thoes who thouht he might make a speach of vengance aganst sin did not acurately know their man. "I addmit weakness in myself," he began. "He who alows it in himself must surely allow it in others."

SPECIAL WORD SECTION—RELIGION

The words listed below appear frequently in articles about religion and in any printed material dealing with subjects involving religious problems. Often these words are misspelled. Master their spelling; then test your knowledge of their *spelling* and *meaning* in the exercise that follows.

atheism	disciple
baptism	gospel
Bible	Judaism
blasphemy	Mohammedanism
Buddhism	orthodox
catechism	parable
Christianity	parochial
congregation	prophet
crucifixion	sacrilegious
deity	theology

Special Word Exercise No. 10

Complete the following sentences by choosing the appropriate word from the list below. *If any word in the list is incorrectly spelled, correct it.*

I.

1. Followers of both ...... and ......
rely upon the ...... as their principal
religious text.
2. ......, a religion of the Far East, is
more mystical than ......, a religion of
the Near East.

> Bibble, Buddism, Judyism,
> Christainity, Mohammedenism

II.

1. The ...... man of faith regards the
disrespectful, ... expressions of
...... as unforgivable examples of
...... against the ....

> diety, athiesm, sacreligious,
> orthodox, blasphimy

III.

1. In the New Testament, ... really
means "good news."
2. In Christianity, the principles of faith
are taught by ......, a rigorous
method of question and answer.
3. Purification by water immersion is
known as ....
4. Schools of ...... staffed by instruc-
tors who have had intensive training in
...... subjects such as religious ethics,
religious literature, and religious history.

> baptizm, catichesim, gospel,
> theologgy, parocheal

IV.

1. ...... as a method of execution was
not new in Jesus' time.
2. The ...... of Israel frequently spoke
to their ...... by means of ......,
simple stories with religious and moral
significance.
3. Each ...... of Jesus had a particular
mission to accomplish.

> congrigation, disiple, crucifiction,
> prophits, parrable

CHAPTER TWELVE

HOMONYMS: PROBLEM PARTNERS

CORE LIST

accuser	calendar	mere
accuses	device	moral
accusing	cigarette	morale
adolescence	cite	morally
adolescent	correlate	off
altogether	difficult	peace
all together	dilemma	permanent
already	dining	phase
amount	disillusioned	prophecy
and	due	scene
annual	except	source
annually	hear	symbol
anticipate	here	where
apologized	ingenious	whole
apology	later	whose
brilliance	loose	quiet
brilliant	loss	

This chapter contains an alphabetical glossary of *homonyms*—words *similar* (though not necessarily identical) in sound but different in meaning and often in spelling. Such words obviously create innumerable spelling as well as usage problems. Many of the words in this glossary have already appeared in this book— on core lists and in exercises. Gathered together, they demonstrate clearly and vividly the similarities and differences that confuse the doubtful speller. To simplify your task these study aids have been included:

1. Definitions of each word.
2. Sentences showing each word in context.
3. Exercises after each group of twenty words.

access	way of approach, admission
excess	superabundance
	General Smith, in an **excess** of generosity, gave enlisted men **access** to the Officer's Club.
accept	to take what is offered
except	(as verb) to exclude
	Edward was willing to accept all invitations, but all **excepted** him from their invitations.
adjoin	to lie next to
adjourn	to suspend a session
	When the judge **adjourns** court for a recess, he retires to his office which **adjoins** the courtroom.
adverse	unfortunate, opposed to
averse	disliking, unwilling
	Because the novel had received **adverse** reviews, he was **averse** to reading it.
advice	(noun, pronounced as *ice*) opinion, recommendation
advise	(verb, pronounced as *ize*) to offer an opinion or a course of action
	I **advise** you to accept my **advice**.
affect	(verb) to act upon, to influence

effect	(noun) result, consequence	assent	to agree, consent

effect   (noun) result, consequence

The **effect** of today's stock market collapse will **affect** my future plans.

HINT: **affect** may serve also as a noun: "feeling, emotion, desire."

effect may serve also as a verb: "to accomplish, to produce."

Unpleasant **affects** may encourage one to **effect** a change in habits.

aisle   passageway

isle   island

There are more **aisles** in Radio City Music Hall than there are **isles** in Jamaica Bay.

all ready   everything is ready

already   previously

We had **already** been at the pier for an hour when the skipper cried, "**All ready**, let's shove off."

all together   everyone in company

altogether   completely, without exception

The club was **altogether** agreed that they should attend the party **all together**.

allusion   a reference

illusion   a false impression, deception

By his repeated **allusions** to the Bible, the imposter created the **illusion** of devoutness.

altar   (noun) a place of worship

alter   (verb) to change

With its newly raised funds the congregation voted to **alter** the **altar**.

angel   a celestial being

angle   a geometric figure

Angels—whether heavenly or human—are delicately shaped rather than harshly **angled**.

ascent   a rising, a going up

assent   to agree, consent

The hikers **assented** to having a guide lead them on their **ascent** of Mt. Glob.

berth   bed (usually on a vehicle); situation; ship's anchorage

birth   act of being born

A Pullman **berth** makes an awkward place for **childbirth**.

beside   at the side of

besides   additionally

None spoke **besides** me; none stood **beside** me—I was alone in the stadium.

brake   a device to arrest motion by friction

break   to separate violently into parts

To **break** your neck while driving an automobile can be simplified if you do not apply your **brakes** at the proper time.

bridal   pertaining to a bride

bridle   headgear used to control a horse

Bridal ceremonies might be enlivened were the groom to apply a **bridle** to his beloved's neck.

Britain   the kingdom of Great Britain

Briton   an Englishman, inhabitant of Great Britain

In Great **Britain,** natives are called **Britons.**

Calvary   a hill near Jerusalem where Jesus was crucified

cavalry   soldiers mounted on horses

The Roman soldiers who accompanied Jesus to his crucifixion at **Calvary** were infantry, not **cavalry.**

capitol   building in which a legislature meets

capital   (used for all other purposes of spelling)

Congress meets in the **capitol** in Washington, D.C., the **capital** of the United States.

Exercise No. 36

Underline the correct word in each of the following sentences.

1. In January, Bill reserved a (birth, berth) on the *Queen Mary* for the following September.
2. Sophia wore an exquisite (bridle, bridal) gown.
3. Bert's appetite was such that six hamburgers at a sitting were not an (excess, access).
4. Stephen would never (assent, ascent) to climbing Pike's Peak on foot.
5. No respectable (Britain, Briton) would (accept, except) coffee at tea-time.
6. Joe's suggestion to rebuild the state (capital, capitol) is a (capital, capitol) one.
7. Marvin will have to (altar, alter) his ways before that girl will marry him.
8. Sherwood has no (allusions, illusions) about women; he knows them to be sweet, understanding, and charitable.
9. Valerie is (adverse, averse) to following her parents' (advice, advise).
10. Sid's interest in money has no (effect, affect) upon me, but I am (altogether, all together) (affected, effected) by his insistence that I stand (beside, besides) him as he counts it.

cite	to quote or refer
sight	(noun) a view; (verb) to see, aim
site	location, situation

When we **sight** the Statue of Liberty, the guide will **cite** pertinent facts about this famed **site**.

climactic	pertaining to or forming the highest point (climax)
climatic	pertaining to or depending upon the weather

The **climactic** event of the journey occurred among the geographic and **climatic** wonders of Mount Everest.

coarse	unrefined, gross
course	(used for all other purposes of spelling)

As a matter of **course**, hostesses exclude **coarse** guests from their receptions.

council	group of people organized to consider affairs
counsel	(noun) advice; (verb) to advise

The Security **Council** met to consider what **counsel** to offer the disputing parties.

crochet	a form of needlework (also a verb)
crotchet	a perverse fancy

Some athletes have strange **crotchets**: one football player I know likes to **crochet** while he sits on the bench.

croquet	a lawn game
croquette	a fried mass of minced meat

A **croquet** mallet would make hash of a chicken **croquette**.

deprecate	to disapprove (usually, with regret)
depreciate	to lessen the price or value of a thing or person

He **deprecated** the growing tendency to **depreciate** learning.

decent	fit, suitable
descent	act of descending or going down

It was **decent** of our guide to allow us to rest during the arduous **descent** from the mountain peak.

dessert	a sweet served after the main course of a meal	fourth	number after *third;* one of four equal parts
desert	(used for all other purposes of spelling: as a noun, the accent is on the first syllable; as a verb, the accent is on the last syllable)		Abel was the **fourth** member of the little family in Eden, but he was not among them when the angel led the family **forth** from Eden.
	Let no one **desert** the dinner table before we have served our special **dessert** of Nesselrode pie.	formally	in a formal manner
		formerly	previously
device	(noun, pronounced as *ice*) an object		We had met **formerly**—three years ago to be exact—but at that time we were not introduced to each other **formally.**
devise	(verb, pronounced as *ize*) to plan, invent, make	foul	ugly, evil
		fowl	a winged bird
	In his laboratory the engineer **devises** plans that lead to the manufacture of **devices** intended to simplify daily living.		All **fowl,** whether chicken, pheasant, or peacock, are to me the **foulest** of creatures.
dining	eating (pronounce first *i* as *eye*)	hoard	(noun) a store laid up; (verb) to lay up a store
dinning	making a loud noise (pronounce first *i* as in *hit*)	horde	a crowd, pack
	The **dinning** of tableware banged to the floor disturbed the quiet of the elegant **dining** room.		When they heard that clocks were to be rationed, the **horde** descended on the jeweler, eager to be there in time to acquire a **hoard** of timepieces.
elicit	to draw out	idle	lazy, doing nothing
illicit	unlawful	idol	a pagan god
	The judge sought to **elicit** details of their **illicit** contract.	idyll	a poem or prose work describing the joys of country life
emigrant	one who *leaves* one country to enter another		**Idle** poets while away their time penning **idylls** in tribute to Pan, the pagan **idol** of the countryside.
immigrant	one who *enters* one country from another	ingenious	clever (pronounce *e* as in *eat*)
	Every **immigrant** must first have been an **emigrant.**	ingenuous	simple, forthright, naive (pronounce *e* as in *hen; u* as in *you*)
eminent	celebrated, conspicuous		An **ingenious** young lady may succeed in convincing an innocent young man that her **ingenuous** remarks about marriage intend him no harm.
imminent	impending, likely to occur at any moment		
	Isaiah, the **eminent** prophet, warned his people of **imminent** disaster.		
forth	onward		

Exercise No. 37

Underline the correct word in each of the following sentences.

1. A (coarse, course) diet best suits an athlete.
2. (Imminent, Eminent) citizens frequently utter (ingenious, ingenuous) remarks which shock their listeners.
3. We are seeking a new (cite, sight, site) on which to build our summer home.
4. I hesitate to (deprecate, depreciate) her specially prepared (desert, dessert).
5. The (council, counsel) (counciled, counseled) that we adopt a (device, devise) to lower prices.
6. Must you lie (idyll, idol, idle) while others sally (fourth, forth) to struggle?
7. I will not play (croquet, croquette) with one who has so many (crotchets, crochets) as Mrs. VanGlump.
8. The killing of the (foul, fowl) was the (climactic, climatic) moment of my stay at the farm.
9. Watching the (immigrants', emigrants') (descent, decent) from the gangplank brought tears to the eyes of the throng.
10. While we are (dinning, dining), I should like to (elicit, illicit) certain information from you.

lead	(noun) a metal (rhymes with *head*)
led	(verb) past tense of the verb *to lead*
	The miners **led** us through the **lead** mine.
loose	(adjective) not tightly fastened; (verb) to free (rhymes with *goose*)
lose	to suffer the loss of (rhymes with *whose*)
	After we **loosed** the kite, we worried that we might **lose** it.

moral	ethical, pertaining to right conduct
morale	mental attitude, usually related to confidence, enthusiasm, and the like.
	When the **morale** of an army is high, its leaders can trust that the **moral** behavior of the men will be sound.
passed	past tense of the verb *to pass*
past	referring to an earlier time
	We have **passed** the stage at which we can ignore the meaning of **past** events.
peace	freedom from disturbance
piece	a portion
	If you expect to have **peace** in this house, you had better listen while I give you a **piece** of my mind.
personal	belonging to a particular person (accent the first syllable *-per'*)
personnel	people engaged in a service (accent the last syllable *-nel'*)
	Mr. Jones, the **personnel** supervisor, takes **personal** interest in the people he hires.
plain	(adjective) simple; (noun) a level, open stretch of land
plane	(adjective) level, flat; (noun) flat surface; tool; social level
	When a **plain** girl seeks to improve her social **plane**, she must improve both her dress and her speech.
principal	chief
principle	rule of conduct or action
	His **principal** objection to women is that they act as their emotions and not as their **principles** impel them to act.
quiet	calm, still (pronounce as *two* syllables: qui et)

quite	entirely, truly (pronounce as *one* syllable) In the **quiet** of his chambers he felt **quite** peaceful.
rain	water
rein	device used to guide horses
reign	rule of a government To **reign** at all, a tyrant must check and **rein** his subjects like horses, if necessary force them to drink **rain** water from puddles.
respectfully	with respect
respectively	each in turn Each candidate **respectively** was called to address the audience. Each began by turning to the chairman and addressing him **respectfully.**
right	correct
rite	ceremony
write	to set down in writing When the journalist began to **write** the story about the wedding **rites**, he made certain that he had all names **right.**
stationary	fixed position
stationery	writing materials When I place **stationery** on my desk and try to compose a letter, I become so nervous that I can't remain **stationary** long enough to think of an opening sentence.
straight	not curved or crooked
strait	(adjective) narrow, strict; (noun) a narrow passageway; difficulty Ships sail a **straight** path on their way to the **Straits** of Magellan.
than	conjunction used to introduce the second item in a comparison
then	at that time When I first saw them together, I knew **then** that she was taller **than** he.
threw	past tense of *to throw*
through	from one side to the other; finished Egbert **threw** the ball **through** Jed's window.
to	(preposition)
too	(adverb) more than enough
two	the number after one On your way home, go **to** the store and buy **two** bars of soap, and a loaf of bread **too.**
vain	egotistical
vein	blood vessel; a distinctive quality of thought or speech, etc.
vane	a pointer So **vain** was Jurgen about his new weathervane that the **veins** in his forehead seemed to puff out as far as his chest.
weak	not strong
week	seven days At the end of a **week** of study I am **weak** with fatigue.
weather	climate
whether	conjunction introducing an alternative **Whether** we go to the ballgame depends entirely on what the **weather** is like.
whose	(possessive pronoun)
who's	contraction of *who is* **Who's** taking **whose** sister to the prom?
your	(possessive pronoun)
you're	contraction of *you are* **You're** taking **your** sister to the dance.

Exercise No. 38

Underline the correct word in each of the following sentences.

1. The (reign, rein, rain) of George III was notable for the absence of (morals, morales) among the ladies of the court.
2. I have been (led, lead) by the nose (too, to, two) easily by (quite, quiet) women.
3. What is the (principle, principal) issue in deciding the (piece, peace) treaty?
4. Craddock has (personal, personnel) reasons for not disclosing his (passed, past) activities.
5. I (respectively, respectfully) submit that I have every (rite, right, write) to use the office (stationary, stationery) for my correspondence.
6. Nan grew up on the midwestern (plain, plane) but since then she has (led, lead) a different sort of life in the city.
7. I know (whose, who's) to blame.
8. (Your, You're) a (weak, week)-minded fellow now just as you were (than, then).
9. If you knew that the diamond he (threw, through) in the corner was there, why did you not walk (strait, straight) to it?
10. When I (loose, lose) my temper, the (vanes, veins, vains) in my temple swell.

Mastery Test Number 11

Do not proceed to the next chapter until you have taken this test. Master the spelling of these words from the *core list* before you try to learn those in the next and final chapter. Remember: in spelling your goal is a perfect score.

I. Choose the appropriate word for each blank. Note that in some instances though all the parenthetic words are correctly spelled, only one is appropriate in context.

1. Hush! Twilight has just fallen and all is (all ready, already) (quite, quiet).
2. (All together, Altogether) there were six of us harmoniously working (all together, altogether).
3. I am unable to (sight, site, cite) for you a single (devise, device) that will make all your decisions.
4. The train was (do, due) at six o'clock and would have arrived (accept, except) that it was derailed.
5. Now (here, hear) this, all of you gathered (hear, here) before me.
6. When his diabolically (ingenious, ingenuous) plan failed, the mad scientist began at once a method which he felt would work at a (later, latter) time.
7. I was at a (lose, loss, loose) to explain his (lose, loss, loose) moral code.
8. Does a low (moral, morale) standard improve (morale, moral) or lower it?
9. Can a prophet (prophesy, prophecy) (piece, peace), or is a (prophecy, prophesy) of that kind merely guesswork?
10. The (whole, hole) (seen, scene) was a shambles when the bomb exploded.

II. Match the core list word with the appropriate context. If the core list word is misspelled, correct it.

	Column A	Column B
1.	I am no longer enchanted	a. symbal
2.	I expect that to happen	b. accusser
3.	The flag means more than a bit of cloth	c. adolesent
4.	He says that I stole the money	d. anual
5.	Check the date	e. anticipate
6.	It happens every year	f. appology
7.	He is not yet an adult	g. pernament
8.	I don't know what to do	h. calander

9. It will last forever
10. I'm sorry

i. dillema
j. disillusioned

III. Each of the core list words in the following sentences needs an extra letter to make it correct. Add the necessary letter.

1. His errant acts make him moraly suspect.
2. When a wife acuses her husband of bad faith, he had better have a ready answer.
3. Adolesence is one of the most painful but exciting periods of life.
4. Annualy, at the end of each year, the company issues its financial report.
5. The pianist gave a briliant performance of Mozart's concerto.
6. May I have a cigarete?
7. How can one corelate vocabulary with intelligence?
8. I find learning spelling rules not as dificult as I had expected.
9. I fell of the pier into the water.
10. I have asked repeatedly whos book this is.

IV. Proofread the following passage, correcting all errors in spelling.

Having concluded his latest fase—accussing his friends of faithlessness—Gerard appologised, explaining that he never knew wher the sourse of his moods was. An, furthermore, he added, a man of his brillance ought not be held accountable for mear rudeness, whether in discussing the ammount of a bill or the guests assembled at the dinning table.

SPECIAL WORD SECTION— RECENT WORDS

The words listed below appear frequently in articles and books about contemporary politics, science, medicine, and the like. Often these words are misspelled. Master their spelling; then test your knowledge of their *spelling* and *meaning* in the exercise that follows.

aggression	hypertension
antihistamine	jet propulsion
barbiturate	nylon
collage	penicillin
documentary	prefabricate
existentialism	racism
extrasensory	streamlined
fissionable	streptomycin
frequency modulation	technological
genocide	telecast

Special Word Exercise No. 11

Complete the following sentences by choosing the appropriate word from the list below. *If any word in the list is incorrectly spelled, correct it.*

I.

1. To ease the stress of ......, doctors occasionally recommend a ...... to sedate a patient's nerves.
2. Three of the most recent "wonder" drugs are ......, ..., and ....

streptimycin, pencillin, barbitchurate, antihistimine, highpertension

II.

1. When rocket aircraft, operated by ...... achieve speeds beyond that of sound, nations must reconsider before they attempt ...... against their neighbors.
2. Hydrogen bombs are constructed of ...... materials which explode with incredible force.
3. ......—prejudice against one of another color, and ......—extermination of a cultural, racial, or political group

represent two of the most heinous evils man has yet to eliminate.

> raceism, aggresion, genocide, jet propellsion, fissionible

III.

1. Last night's . . . . . presented a straightforward, factual . . . . . . about the manufacture of . . . . . . stockings.
2. . . . . . ., better known as FM, produces clearer radio reception than ordinary, or AM reception.
3. Making a . . . . . . can be fun. Just paste on a sheet of paper bits of colored cloth, paper clips, newspaper fragments and the like.

> collage, documentery, telecast, nilon, frequency modulaition

IV.

1. Improved . . . . . . methods have enabled industry to produce . . . . . houses —practically ready-made—whose . . . . appearance appeals to both practical and esthetic senses.
2. . . . . . . has gained followers in the United States as well as in France where its proponents insist that man alone is responsible for what he is.
3. Certain schools of psychology insist that many of man's perceptions need to be explained as . . . . . . rather than as dependent upon what his senses experience.

> extrasensery, existentielism, technilogical, streamlined, prefabrecated

CHAPTER THIRTEEN

WORD SAVERS: MEMORY DEVICES

CORE LIST

absence	cemetery	hopeless
abundance	children	hoping
abundant	competitor	huge
acclaim	competition	hundred
accustom	dealt	idea
actual	dissatified	laid
actuality	divide	literature
actually	divine	maybe
adequate	dropped	medicine
adequately	during	plausible
advertiser	easily	politician
advertising	eighth	practice
advertisement	entertainment	presence
another	escape	safety
apparatus	especially	sentence
appreciate	every	themselves
area	genius	

Throughout this book you have learned that the word to be spelled is more important than any rule. Nevertheless, by an intelligent application of certain useful principles of spelling, pronunciation, and word formation, you have already mastered the spelling of a considerable number of troublesome words. In this, the final chapter of the book, you can learn how to add certain *memory devices* to your arsenal of weapons to combat weak spelling.

Memory devices (technically, *mnemonics*, from Greek, "to remember") are techniques of memory association. They differ from the prin-

ciples you have already learned because they are *personal* rather than general in application. The device that works perfectly for Mr. Jones may prove worthless for Mr. Smith. But if your memory device works for you, use it. Never mind if the other fellow thinks it silly. The wisest generalization to follow when thinking about memory devices is this: *Keep the device simple.* It is easier to learn to spell the word than to memorize the device. With this observation in mind, you may find the following techniques helpful.

1. Wherever possible, reduce the troublesome word to simple words.

> sergeant—**serge ant**
> battalion—**batta**(atta boy)**lion**
> business—**sin in business**
> separate—**pa rate** (or **rat**)
> jewelry—**jewel in jewelry**
> balloon—**ball in balloon**
> tenant—**ten ant**
> costume—**cost in costume**
> together—**to get her**
> modern—**mode in modern**
> physician—**physic in physician**
> repetition—**pet in repetition**
> recommend—**commend** in r**e**command
> maintenance—**main ten ance**
> candidate—**candid ate**

2. Break the word into syllables and pronounce

each syllable—even if the word is not normally pronounced that way. (Use your dictionary to learn how each of the following words is actually pronounced.)

hand ker chief	extra ordinary
fore head	li e u ten ant
lab o ra tory	post hu mous
or chest ra	hand some

3. Associate the word with its origin.

kindergarten —from German **kinder**, "children," and **garten**, "garden."

tragedy —from Greek **tragos**, "goat,"
tragic probably a reference to the half-man, half-goat creatures who attended Bacchus, the god in whose honor **tragedy** is supposed to have originated.

cafeteria —from French **café**, "coffee."

paraphernalia—from Greek **para**, "besides," and **pherne**, "dowry," in reference to an early marital custom that gave wives legal right to all property except their dowry.

exorbitant —from Latin **ex**, "out of," and **orb**, "world"—in other words, exorbitant prices are "out of this world."

What memory devices can you create for the following words? Use your dictionary to find their origins: pandemonium, glamor, grammar, enigmatic, boudoir.

4. Create your own tricks. Anything goes:

cemetery   We get there with ease (E's)

experience }
existence }   These are Easy words

develop   **Lop** off the final e

grammar   Write **gram**, then spell it backwards, but drop the **g**.

indispensable   That which one is not **able** to **dispense** with.

hear   **hear** with your **ear**
here   **here** is **where** you are
principle   A princip**LE** is a ru**LE**

HINT: Try applying mnemonic devices to the list of homonyms in Chapter Twelve.

Mastery Test Number 12

This is the final Mastery Test. Do not proceed to the Final Review Test of Core List Words until you have taken this test. Some of the words from this Mastery Test may appear on that review test. Once more, remember: in spelling your goal is a perfect score.

I. Match the core list word with the appropriate context. If the core list word is misspelled, correct it.

Column A	*Column B*
1. We have plenty of everything	a. apparetus
2. He deserves our applause	b. hunderd
3. That will be satisfactory	c. abundence
4. Bury the dead	d. advertissing
5. Get them to buy our product	e. aclaim
6. Beat the other fellow	f. adequate
7. His talent is extraordinary	g. hugge
8. An enormous truck	h. compitition
9. In years, a century	i. ccmetary
10. Will this device work?	j. genuis

II. One letter in each of the italicized words is incorrect. Substitute the correct letter.
   1. *Absense* makes the heart grow fonder.
   2. An *abundent* harvest will make the farmers happy.
   3. He performs his tasks *adaquately*.
   4. Send your material to the *advertisor* and he will write the copy.

5. I *appresiate* your efforts in my behalf.
6. We must find a way to outsell our *competetor*.
7. A house must not *devide* against itself.
8. Prisoners rarely *excape* from their cells.
9. I fail to get your *idear*.
10. The druggist will send the *medecine* to your home shortly.

III. One word in each of the following groups is correctly spelled. Choose the word.

1. I cannot (acustom, accustom, accusstom) myself to her face.
2. Did he (actually, actualy, actully) arrive on time?
3. I placed an (advertizement, advertisment, advertisement) in the newspaper.
4. Ask the (childern, childeren, children) to eat in their own room.
5. I am (hopeing, hopping, hoping) that you will be our guest for tea.
6. We are quite (disatisfied, dissatisfied, dissatisfied) with our room service.
7. Your red hat is an (especially, especially, especialy) attractive one.

8. The study of (litrature, litterature, literature) is arduous but rewarding.
9. In the (presence, presense, prescence) of his neighbors, he kissed his wife.
10. We live on the (eigth, eihth, eighth) floor.

IV. Proofread the following passages, correcting all errors in spelling.

A. To succeed, a musical comedy must provide entertaiment. Durring the show the actors must seem to enjoy themselfs; they must deliver lines to one annother easely and naturally; everry moment must suggest that this play is the finished product of months of actul practise and rehearsal. Mebbe then the play will flourish even if the soprano's voice is not devine.

B. The pollitician in my araea is a plausable fellow of high sentance. He has dropped mighty words about public safty and layed several cornerstones. But in actuallity he has delt with no significant issue; he has, in brief, proved himself to be a hopless incompetent.

FINAL TESTS

The *Final Review Test* in Part I contains the same fifty words from the core list which were used at the outset of this book on the *Pre-Test*. If you find that your score is perfect—as it should be—do not assume that your task is over, though you are now securely on your way. Spelling needs continuous attention. Continue to review. Construct your own tests. Use your newly mastered words in context. From time to time, test yourself on the *Mastery Tests* in this book. Your attitude toward spelling has much to do with your continued improvement. Accept the challenge and responsibility that are yours. The rewards are immense —and it can be great fun.

Part I: Underline the one correctly spelled word in each of the following groups.

1. loseing, losing, lossing
2. proceed, procede, proseed, prosede
3. hieght, heighth, height, hieghth
4. oppinion, opinion, opinnion, oppinnion
5. writing, writeing, writting, writteing
6. proffessor, profesor, proffesor, professor
7. therefor, therefore, therfor, therfore
8. forlegn, forein, forien, foreign
9. marraige, marridge, marriage, marrage
10. all right, alright, allright, all rite
11. heros, heroez, heroes, herroes
12. refered, referred, reffered, refferred
13. amachoor, amatoor, amatur, amateur
14. atheist, athiest, atheast, athaest
15. ninty, ninety, ninedy, ninnety
16. advertisement, advertizment, advertisment, advertizement
17. leasure, leesure, leisure, liesure
18. labratory, laborattory, laboratory, labaratory
19. irestistible, irresistable, irresisible, iresisttible
20. discription, description, descripttion, discripttion
21. efficeint, eficient, eficeint, efficient
22. rhythm, rythm, ryrhm, rhytm
23. embarass, embarrass, emberress, emmbarass
24. enviroment, environent, environment, envirronment
25. exaggerate, exagerate, exagerrate, exegarrate
26. prevalent, privelant, prevelant, prevelent
27. irrevelant, irrelevent, irrelevant, irelevant
28. ocurence, occurance, occurence, occurrence
29. accidently, accidentaly, accidentally, accidentilly
30. adolesence, adolecense, adolesense, adolescense
31. wierd, weard, weird, weiard
32. advantagous, advantageous, advanttagous, addvantageous
33. paralel, parralel, parallel, paralell
34. imediately, imeddiatcly, immediately, immcdiatly
35. beneficcial, benefficial, beneficail, beneficial
36. criticism, criticizm, critticism, critticizm
37. occassion, occasion, ocassion, ocasion
38. lonliness, lonelyness, loneliness, lonlyness
39. charcteristic, chrackteristic, characteristic, characteristick
40. beleif, beleaf, belief, bellief
41. acomodate, accomadate, acommodate, accommodate
42. disapoint, disappoint, dissappoint, disapoint

99

43. grammer, gramar, grammar, gramer
44. athelete, atlete, athleet, athlete
45. intrest, interest, interrest, intirest
46. controversial, contraversial, controversail, contriversial
47. separite, seperate, separate, sepparate
48. maintainance, maintenance, maintenence, maintainence
49. arguement, argumment, argument, arrgument
50. villein, villain, villian, villin

Part II: Underline the one correctly spelled word in each of the following groups. The following words have been taken from exercises 25-38.

1. amirable, admirible, admirable, admirrable
2. alyin, alien, alein, allien
3. auxiliary, auxilary, auxilliery, auxiliery
4. averse, averce, avoice, averrse
5. beir, bier, biere, beire
6. breef, breif, breaf, brief
7. Britton, Brittan, Briton, briton
8. casheer, casheir, cashier, cashear
9. cieling, ceiling, cealing, sieling
10. civilian, civilien, civillian, civillain
11. climacktic, climactic, climactik, climectic
12. countarfiet, counterfiet, counterfeit, counterfiat
13. couragous, courageous, courageious, couragus
14. crotchet, crotchit, crotchat, crochit
15. decietful, deceitfull, deceitful, deceatful
16. deign, deagn, daegn, diegn
17. deprecate, depresate, depprecate, depracate

18. desireable, desirrable, desirable, dessirable
19. duely, duly, dooly, dooley
20. eether, eather, either, eyether
21. ilicit, elicit, ellicit, elisit
22. excede, exseed, exceed, exsede
23. exsess, exscess, excess, ekcess
24. facetshous, facetious, fascetious, facetus
25. fiegn, faign, feign, fein
26. feind, fiend, feand, feend
27. fierce, fearce, feirce, feerce
28. fiary, feiry, fiery, fyery
29. gayety, gaiety, gaeity, gayty
30. glashier, glacier, glaceir, glacer
31. greef, grief, greif, greaf
32. likable, likible, likeible, likeable
33. medeval, medeival, medieval, mediaval
34. meen, mein, mien, mian
35. misscheif, mischeif, mischief, mischeef
36. movaible, movable, moveible, movvable
37. naybor, neighbor, niegbor, neigbor
38. neether, neyether, neather, neither
39. outragous, outragious, outrageous, outrageus
40. patient, patiant, pattient, pashient
41. peaceable, peacable, paseable, peaceible
42. picnicing, picniking, picnicking, picniccing
43. peir, pier, peeir, pire
44. profficient, proficient, profishient, proficeint
45. reppreive, repreave, reprieve, repreive
46. siezure, seizure, seasure, seazure
47. slaigh, sliegh, sleigh, slegh
48. straight, streight, striaght, straigt
49. trolleis, trolleys, trollies, troleys
50. paniced, paniked, panicked, panicced

APPENDIX A

COMPREHENSIVE CORE LIST

Listed below in **alphabetical** order are the 500 **core list** words. For your convenience the chapter in which each word appears has been noted.

absence, 13
abundance, 13
abundant, 13
academic, 8
academically, 8
academy, 8
accept, 8
acceptable, 8
acceptance, 8
accepting, 8
access, 8
accessible, 8
accident, 8
accidental, 8
accidentally, 8
acclaim, 13
accommodate, 2
accompanied, 10
accompanies, 10
accompaniment, 10
accompanying, 10
accomplish, 11
accuracy, 11
accurate, 11
accurately, 11
accuser, 12
accuses, 12
accusing, 12
accustom, 13
achieve, 2
achievement, 2
acquaint, 4
acquaintance, 4
across, 8
actual, 13
actuality, 13
actually, 13
adequate, 13
adequately, 13
admission, 11

admit, 11
admittance, 11
adolescence, 12
adolescent, 12
advantage, 10
advantageous, 10
advertiser, 13
advertising, 13
advertisement, 13
advice, 5
advise, 5
affect, 3
afraid, 11
against, 11
aggravate, 11
aggressive, 7
alleviate, 11
allotment, 11
allotted, 11
allow, 11
allowed, 11
allows, 11
all right, 2
altar, 11
altogether, 12
all together, 12
already, 12
amateur, 11
among, 3
amount, 12
analysis, 5
analyze, 5
and, 12
annual, 12
annually, 12
another, 13
anticipate, 12
apologized, 12
apology, 12
apparatus, 13

apparent, 5
appear, 5
appearance, 5
applies, 10
applying, 10
appreciate, 13
approach, 5
approaches, 5
area, 13
arguing, 7
argument, 7
arise, 6
arising, 6
article, 8
atheist, 9
athlete, 3
athletic, 3
attendance, 9
attendant, 9
attended, 9
author, 9
authoritative, 9
authority, 9

basically, 8
basis, 8
before, 9
began, 3
begin, 3
beginning, 3
belief, 2
believe, 2
beneficial, 3
benefit, 3
benefited, 3
brilliance, 12
brilliant, 12
Britain, 8
Britannica, 8
buried, 10
bury, 10
business, 2
busy, 2

calendar, 12
careful, 9

careless, 9
carried, 10
carrier, 10
carries, 10
carrying, 10
category, 4
cemetery, 13
challenge, 8
changeable, 10
changing, 10
character, 6
characteristic, 6
characterize, 6
chief, 9
children, 13
choice, 3
choose, 3
chose, 3
Christ, 8
Christian, 8
Christianity, 8
cigarette, 12
cite, 12
coming, 8
companies, 10
company, 10
comparative, 4
competitor, 13
competition, 13
concede, 11
conceivable, 6
conceive, 6
condemn, 3
connotation, 10
connote, 10
conscience, 4
conscientious, 4
conscious, 4
consider, 6
considerably, 6
consistency, 5
consistent, 5
continuous, 11
control, 7
controlled, 7
controversial, 4

controversy, 4
convenience, 6
convenient, 6
correlate, 12
council, 10
counsel, 10
counselor, 10
countries, 10
criticism, 2
criticize, 2
curiosity, 8
curious, 8

dealt, 13
deceive, 9
decided, 8
decision, 8
define, 2
definite, 2
definitely, 2
definition, 2
dependent, 9
describe, 4
description, 4
desirability, 10
desire, 10
device, 12
difference, 6
different, 6
difficult, 12
dilemma, 12
dining, 12
disappoint, 6
disastrous, 3
disciple, 8
discipline, 8
disillusioned, 12
dissatisfied, 13
divide, 13
divine, 13
doesn't, 8
dominant, 6
dropped, 13
due, 12
during, 13

easily, 13
effect, 3
effective, 3
efficiency, 6
efficient, 6
eighth, 13
embarrass, 5
entertain, 9
entertainment, 13
environment, 3

escape, 13
especially, 13
etc., 8
every, 13
exaggerate, 4
except, 12
exercise, 6
exist, 2
existence, 2
existent, 2
experience, 4
explanation, 4
extremely, 10

familiar, 8
field, 9
finally, 8
financially, 9
financier, 9
foreign, 5
foreigners, 5
forty, 2
fourth, 2
friend, 9
friendliness, 9
fulfil(l), 7
fundamental, 8
fundamentally, 8
further, 7

gaiety, 9
genius, 13
government, 3
governor, 3
grammar, 5
guidance, 6

happiness, 9
hear, 12
height, 5
here, 12
hero, 5
heroes, 5
heroic, 5
heroine, 5
hindrance, 7
hopeless, 13
hoping, 13
huge, 13
humor, 7
humorist, 7
humorous, 7
hundred, 13
hypocrisy, 7
hypocrite, 7

idea, 13
imaginary, 5
imagination, 5
imagine, 5
immediate, 4
immediately, 4
incident, 4
incidentally, 4
independent, 6
independence, 6
influence, 9
influential, 9
ingenious, 12
intelligent, 4
interest, 3
interpret, 3
interpretation, 3
involve, 9
irrelevant, 6
irresistible, 6
irritable, 6
its, 2
it's, 2

knowledge, 9

laboratory, 9
laid, 13
later, 12
led, 5
leisure, 9
leisurely, 9
length, 8
lengthening, 8
literature, 13
liveliest, 9
livelihood, 9
liveliness, 9
lives, 9
loneliness, 4
lonely, 4
loose, 12
lose, 2
losing, 2
loss, 12

maintenance, 6
marriage, 3
maybe, 13
medicine, 13
mere, 12
moral, 12
morale, 12
morally, 12
necessary, 4
Negro, 5

Negroes, 5
ninety, 9
noticeable, 4

occasion, 2
occur, 2
occurred, 2
occurrence, 2
occurring, 2
off, 12
omit, 10
omitted, 10
operate, 6
opinion, 6
opponent, 6
opportunity, 6
oppose, 6
optimism, 6
origin, 7
original, 7

paid, 11
parallel, 10
particular, 10
passed, 5
past, 5
peace, 12
perceive, 9
perform, 4
performance, 4
permanent, 12
permit, 10
personal, 3
personnel, 3
phase, 12
philosophy, 7
physical, 11
piece, 9
planned, 11
plausible, 13
pleasant, 11
politician, 13
possess, 4
possession, 4
practice, 13
presence, 13
possible, 11
precede, 6
predominant, 6
prefer, 6
preferred, 6
prejudice, 4
prevalent, 5
principal, 5
principle, 5
privilege, 4

probably, 4
procedure, 6
proceed, 6
profession, 4
professor, 4
prominent, 5
propaganda, 7
propagate, 7
prophecy, 12
psychoanalysis, 7
psychology, 4
psychopathic, 7
pursue, 5

quantity, 11
quiet, 12

really, 2
realize, 2
receive, 2
receiving, 2
recommend, 4
refer, 6
referred, 6
referring, 6
relieve, 9
religion, 11
repetition, 4
response, 11
rhythm, 5
ridicule, 7
ridiculous, 7

safety, 13
satire, 7
satirize, 7
scene, 12
seize, 9
sense, 5
sentence, 13
separate, 2
separation, 2
sergeant, 7
shining, 3
significance, 11
similar, 3
sincerely, 10
sophomore, 7
source, 12
speaking, 8
speech, 11
sponsor, 11
stabilization, 11
strength, 8
stories, 10
story, 10
studying, 5
subtle, 7
succeed, 4
success, 4
sufficient, 10
summary, 7
summed, 7
suppose, 7

suppress, 7
surprise, 3
susceptible, 11
swimming, 10
symbol, 12

technique, 7
temperament, 7
than, 3
their, 2
themselves, 13
then, 3
theories, 10
theory, 10
there, 2
therefore, 7
they're, 2
thorough, 3
those, 11
thought, 11
to, 2
together, 7
tomorrow, 11
too, 2
they're, 2
tragedy, 7
transferred, 10
tremendous, 11
tried, 5
tries, 5
two, 2

tyranny, 7

undoubtedly, 11
unusual, 7
unusually, 7
useful, 4
useless, 4
using, 4

varies, 5
various, 5
vengeance, 11
view, 9
villain, 7

warrant, 11
weather, 3
weird, 9
where, 12
whether, 3
whole, 12
whose, 12
woman, 3
women, 3
write, 3
writer, 3
writing, 3
written, 3

yield, 9
you're, 8

APPENDIX B

TROUBLESOME WORDS

Listed below in alphabetical order are 199 troublesome words—other than core list words—which have been used in exercises throughout this book. To make it simpler for you to review the principles involved in any word, the number of the **exercise** in which the word appears has been noted.

Note: Words from the Special Word Sections appear in **Appendix C.**

admirable, 30
aggrandize, 20
alien, 29
allocate, 14
amicable, 17
antecedent, 15
Arctic, 1
ashen, 7
auxiliary, 37
averse, 38

background, 3
berth, 38
bier, 28
blamable, 17
brief, 29
Briton, 38
buoyant, 5

calf, 8
calves, 8
capital, 38
capitol, 38
cashier, 28
ceiling, 29
chastise, 18
chateau, 9
chocolate, 1
civilian, 37
climactic, 39
college, 4
collegiate, 4
commissioner, 13
competent, 13
consummate, 23
counterfeit, 29

courageous, 31
crises, 10
crisis, 10
crotchet, 39
curable, 17

deceitful, 29
deign, 28
demonstrable, 17
deplorable, 17
deprecate, 39
desirable, 30
despair, 15
divulge, 15
diary, 2
diffident, 23
digress, 14
dilettante, 9
dissimilar, 13
dissonance, 13
district, 3
duly, 31
dwindling, 5
dynamo, 10

efficacious, 20
eider, 29
either, 29
elicit, 38
embargo, 8
exactly, 3
exceed, 37
excess, 38
excessive, 5
expatriate, 20
extravagant, 16

facetious, 24
families, 32
feign, 28
fiend, 28
fierce, 28
fiery, 29
fox, 10
foxes, 10
frivolous, 4

gaiety, 29
glacier, 29
gnus, 7
gratuitous, 23
grief, 29
guardian, 37

heifer, 29
heinous, 28
hesitant, 16
hierarchy, 29
hoof, 8
hoofs, 8

igneous, 23
ignite, 23
ignoble, 14
ignorant, 16
illiterate, 21
illusion, 38
imbibe, 14
immovable, 17
infallible, 21
inference, 16
ingenuous, 39
innuendo, 10
intangible, 17
interference, 16
inveigh, 28
inveigle, 29
invincible, 17
irascible, 17
irrigate, 14

jewels, 2

kissable, 7
knife, 8
knives, 8

likeable, 30
likelihood, 30
liquefy, 18
lynxes, 7

malicious, 23
martial, 37
mathematics, 2
medicinal, 4
medieval, 29
mien, 29
miniature, 2
mischief, 29
mishap, 13
misshapen, 13
mosses, 7
movable, 30
mysterious, 4
mystery, 4

neighbor, 29
neither, 29

omniscient, 29
ostriches, 7
outrageous, 31
ox, 10
oxen, 10

panicked, 37
parliament, 2
partner, 3
passage, 5
patient, 29
peaceable, 37
persist, 15
picnicking, 37
pier, 29
plausible, 17
predictable, 17
priestly, 29
proficient, 29

APPENDIX C

CORE LIST OF SPECIALIZED WORDS

Listed below in **alphabetical** order are the **specialized** words from the Special Word Sections. For easy reference the chapter in which each word appears has been noted.

abacus, 6
abandonment, 3
abstraction, 7
abutments, 10
a capella, 7
accessory, 3
accountant, 2
acknowledgment, 2
adjudicate, 3
adenoids, 5
affidavit, 3
aggression, 12
alibi, 3
alimony, 3
allergy, 5
amnesia, 9
amphibians, 4
amplifier, 6
anatomy, 4
angle, 6
annul, 3
antibiotics, 5
antihistamine, 12
antiseptic, 5
antitoxin, 5
anxiety, 9
aptitude, 9
arabesque, 7
arraign, 3
astigmatism, 5
atheism, 11
atonality, 7
auditor, 2
autobiography, 8

bacilli, 4
bailiff, 3
ballet, 7
bankrupt, 3

baptism, 11
barbiturate, 12
baroque, 10
Bible, 11
bibliography, 8
bigamy, 3
blasphemy, 11
botany, 4
Buddhism, 11
burglary, 3
buttresses, 10
Byzantine, 10

cadence, 7
cantilever, 10
carbohydrate, 4
cardiology, 5
carnivorous, 4
catarrh, 5
catechism, 11
cathode ray, 6
ceramic, 7
chiaroscuro, 7
chlorophyll, 4
choreography, 7
Christianity, 11
chromosome, 4
circumference, 6
classicism, 8
claustrophobia, 9
coercion, 3
collage, 12
collateral, 2
colonnades, 10
comedy, 8
congregation, 11
cornice, 10
corridor, 10
cosmic rays, 6

counsellor-at-law, 3
counterpoint, 7
coupon, 2
crucifixion, 11
cyclotron, 6

decimal, 6
defendant, 3
deity, 11
denominator, 6
diagnosis, 5
disciple, 11
dissonance, 7
documentary, 12
drama, 8
dunning, 2

eczema, 5
electronics, 6
embezzle, 2
embryo, 4
empirical, 9
entrechat, 7
entrepreneur, 2
epilepsy, 5
essay, 8
evolution, 4
existentialism, 12
extrasensory, 12

facade, 10
fidelity, 6
fissionable, 12
franchise, 2
frequency modulation, 12
fugue, 7
fungus, 4

gargoyles, 10
genocide, 12
girder, 10
gospel, 11
Gothic, 10
gouache, 7

hemorrhage, 5
heredity, 4
homicide, 3
hormone, 5
hypertension, 12
hypotenuse, 6
hysteria, 9

imagery, 8
indictment, 3
infinity, 6
inhibitions, 9
inoculate, 5
instinct, 4
integer, 6
intelligence, 9
isosceles, 6

jet propulsion, 12
Judaism, 11

lancet, 10
laryngitis, 5
ledger, 2
liability, 2
liquidate, 2
lyric, 8

madrigal, 7
mammal, 4
management, 2
merchandise, 2
meter (metre), 8
microscope, 4
Mohammedanism, 11
mortgage, 2
mosaic, 10

narrative, 8
naturalism, 9
nave, 10
negotiable, 2
neurosis, 9
novel, 8
nuclear fission, 6

numerator, 6
nylon, 12

obstetrics, 5
Oedipus complex, 9
organism, 4
orthodox, 11

parable, 11
paralysis, 5
paranoid, 9
parasite, 4
parochial, 11
pediatrician, 5
penicillin, 12
perpendicular, 6
personnel, 2
picaresque, 8
pirouette, 7

prefabricated, 12
prologue, 8
promissory, 2
prophet, 11
protoplasm, 4
psychiatry, 9
psychoanalysis, 9
psychosis, 9
psychosomatic, 9

quotient, 6

racism, 12
rapport, 9
realism, 8
repression, 9
rhapsody, 7
rhyme, 8
rhythm, 9

Romanesque, 10
romanticism, 8
rotunda, 10

sacrilegious, 11
satire, 8
senility, 9
soliloquy, 8
staccato, 7
streamlined, 12
streptomycin, 12
subpoena, 3
sublimation, 9
supersonic, 6
surrealism, 7
symphony, 7
syndicate, 2

tariff, 2

technological, 12
telecast, 12
theology, 11
tragedy, 8
transference, 9
trellis, 10

usury, 3

vaccine, 5
veneer, 10
vertebrate, 4
virus, 5

wainscot, 10

writ, 3

zoology, 4

SUPPLEMENT I

PRONUNCIATION

Those of us who wish to improve our speech as well as our spelling want to use correct pronunciations. We want to be considered careful, not careless, in our speech habits; we want to avoid being caught in simple mistakes. We seek the assurance and confidence that comes from knowing we are doing something the right way.

In English, however, there is no such thing as a "correct" pronunciation, in the sense that the answer to an arithmetic problem is correct. There is no *one* right way to say a word. English-speaking peoples have no national academy to determine matters of pronunciation.

Therefore, it is better to think of pronunciations as being acceptable or unacceptable, that is, in good usage or not.

ACCEPTABLE AMERICAN PRONUNCIATION

A pronunciation is acceptable in the United States if it meets the following requirements:

1. If it is native, not foreign. Good English is not spoken with a foreign accent. In any area with large members of immigrants, one must be wary of unconsciously adopting foreignisms.

2. If it is also native, in that it is American, not British. For a person born in the United States to affect a Cockney or an Oxford accent is downright silly.

3. If it is characteristic of some region of the United States, not some small locality, such as a town. Coastal New England, the middle Atlantic area, the coastal and the mountain South, the West, are examples of regions.

A corollary, here, is that no one region is superior to others in pronunciation. A New Yorker should not attempt to talk like a Texan, nor a Texan like a resident of Maine.

4. If it is used by educated and cultured people. We should take as guides those who know something about the language and treat it with respect. We can get little help from those whose vocabulary is meager and who do not care how they say the words they do know.

5. If it is modern. Pronunciations change, and there isn't much sense in adopting a pronunciation last heard 500 years ago or one we think will be popular twenty-five years hence.

A corollary here is that while one need not use the pronunciations of one's grandmother, one should not criticize *her* for using those she was taught.

From these criteria it is clear that more than one pronunciation of a word may be acceptable, that is, in good usage.

A pronunciation may be unacceptable because it is foreign, provincial, pedantic, affected, or obsolete.

THE DICTIONARY AND PRONUNCIATION

A dictionary does not legislate about pronunciation. It records present good usage. It points out choices in pronunciation. It indicates regional variations. It suggests levels on which certain usages are appropriate.

A dictionary, therefore, furnishes the necessary information for a sound judgment as to what is acceptable pronunciation in a given situation. It must be used with care and discrimination.

In learning to use a dictionary:

Familiarize yourself with its symbols indicating pronunciation.

These are listed in a *PRONUNCIATION KEY* or *GUIDE TO PRONUNCIATION* at the beginning of the volume. A short form of the key is usually printed at the top or bottom of all the pages of the text.

Both *WEB* and *ACD* use diacritical markings to indicate pronunciation. The word is re-spelled and certain marks are placed above or below the re-spellings to give the pronunciations more accurately. Thus, in both dictionaries the symbol ā is used for the vowel of *cape, ale, fate.*

You must realize, in following these markings, that your pronunciation will only be as accurate as your interpretation of them. If you mistake the meaning of the marks, your pronunciation will be mistaken. Dictionaries help to guard against this by printing several key words for each diacritical mark in the full key at the beginning of the volume. Refer to these whenever you are in doubt about any sounds.

Make sure you are looking up the right word, the one you want.

Sometimes words are spelled in the same way but have such different meanings that they are printed as separate entries. *Indict,* in the usual sense of "to charge with an offense," has a different pronunciation (in·dīt′ in *WEB*) from *indict,* in the usual sense of "to proclaim" (in·dĭkt′). As a matter of fact, the latter is a common mispronunciation of the word in its usual meaning.

One word may be used as several different parts of speech with possibly different pronunciations (*perfect* as an adjective and a verb). These may be listed together or separately.

In all dictionaries, check the meaning of the word and its part of speech before you look at its pronunciation.

Examine *all* the pronunciations given for a word. Two, three, or more may be offered. The adjective *alternate* has four acceptable pronunciations.

The first listing is usually the most widespread and therefore the preferred pronunciation.

Note the special comments that may be made about particular pronunciations.

Pronunciations may be called British, local, colloquial, provincial, popular, or poetic. The phrases "older," "formerly," and "less often" are also used.

Finally, if the dictionary offers a choice of pronunciations, you should ask your friends for their vote. In general, you should try to conform to the pronunciations of your region.

A NOTE ON THE PRONUNCIATION LISTS

The remainder of this section is devoted largely to pronunciation lists.

These are not intended to be a substitute for a dictionary.

Rather, their purpose is to point out common types of mistakes in pronunciation, to show how these mistakes may be corrected, and to illustrate or emphasize certain principles that will be a help in improving your pronunciation generally.

Practice the lists only in conjunction with, and as illustrations for, the observations which precede them. Take up one list at a time. Read through it, saying aloud both the acceptable and the unacceptable forms. Note particularly those words which you have been mispronouncing. Say the correct pronunciations over several times, trying to fix them in your mind. Say the word in a short sentence. Keep a notebook of such words, and each week try to work three or four into your conversation.

PRONUNCIATION KEY

In the lists that follow, the pronunciations are indicated by a simple system of re-spelling.

Vowels

SYMBOL	KEY WORD	RE-SPELLING
EE	seem	SEEM
AY	say	SAY
Y	buy	BY
OH	no	NOH
OO	ooze	OOZ
AW	taught	TAWT
AH	farm	FAHRM
UR	burn	BURN
OY	toy	TOY
OW	now	NOW
YOO	use	YOOZ
AYR	air	AYR

The remaining vowels are usually indicated by a vowel plus two consonants.

VOWEL	as in	WORD	RE-SPELLING
I		ill	ILL
A		bat	BATT
E		end	ENND
O		hot	HOTT (This sound varies from short AH to short AW.)
U		cup	KUPP

The vowel of *push, pull* is usually indicated by U, and a key word is supplied.

The vowels of unaccented syllables are weak, and have only a part of the quality of the original or else are completely blurred or indeterminate in quality. For these, the original spellings are usually retained: alone (a-LOHN), system (SISS-tem), easily (EE-zi-lee), honor (ONN-or), campus (KAMM-pus).

Consonants

These letters have their usual value: b, d, f, h, k, l, m, n, p, r, s, t, v, w, y (before vowels, as in *yes*), z. The remaining consonants are indicated as follows:

SYMBOL	KEY WORD	RE-SPELLING
G	gay	GAY
J	jay	JAY
TCH	chief	TCHEEF
NG	sing	SING
SH	shoe	SHOO
ZH	measure	MEZH-ur
TH	thin	THINN
TH	than	THANN

NOTE: *W* is used for words spelled with *wh*, since this sound may be a *W*, a voiceless *W*, or an *HW*. *C* is not used, since it may have the sound of *S* or *K*. *Q* is not used, since its sound is *KW*. *X* is not used, since its sound is either *KS* or *GZ*.

Syllables. Syllables are separated by dashes: *finger* (FING-ger). It should be remembered that syllables can be indicated only roughly in English.

Accent. Only the primary accent of a word is given and this is indicated by capitals: *going* (GOH-ing), *demoniacal* (dee-mo-NY-a-kal). The secondary accent is not indicated because it usually does not present a problem.

COMMON MISTAKES IN PRONUNCIATION

Spelling Pronunciations

Certain mistakes in pronunciation are made because the speaker follows spellings too closely.

Sometimes there is good reason for this sort of mistake. Simple, old words may decline in use, or words common to one region may not be used in another. We may not have *heard* these words, and when we *see* them may consider them too simple to look up in a dictionary. These very ordinary words, however, deserve to be correctly pronounced:

WORD	SAY	NOT
ague	AY-gyoo	AYG
awry	a-RY	AW-ree
bade	BAD	BAYD
blackguard	BLAG-ard	BLACK-GAHRD
breeches	BRITCH-iz	BREETCH-iz
comely	KUMM-lee	KOHM-lee
orgy	AWR-jee	AWR-gee (*g* as in *get*)
quay	KEE	KWAY
victuals	VITT-'lz	VIKK-tchoo-'lz

Sometimes the mispronounced words, while not literary, are a bit out of the ordinary. A careful speaker would have looked them up in a dictionary rather than guessed at their pronunciation from the spelling. In the word *misled,* the spelling pronunciation MIZZ-'ld probably occurs only when the word is read aloud.

WORD	SAY	NOT
comptroller	kon-TROH-ler	komp-TROH-ler
culinary	KYOO-li-ner-ee	KULL-i-ner-ee
disheveled	di-SHEVV-eld	diss-HEVV-eld
doughty	DOW-tee	DOH-tee
indict (to charge with a crime)	in-DYT	in-DIKT
longevity	lon-JEV-i-tee	long-GEV-i-tee
misled	miss-LED	MIZZ-'ld
parliamentary	pahr-li-MEN-ter-ee	pahr-lee-a-MEN-ter-ee
piquant	PEE-k'nt	PEE-kwant
solace	SOLL-iss	SOH-liss
subtle	SUTT-'l	SUBB-tel
vehement	VEE-e-mint	VEE-hem-ent
zoology	zoh-OLL-o-jee	ZOO-lo-jee

On the other hand, people occasionally mispronounce ordinary words that they must hear very frequently indeed. It is an extraordinary tribute to the power of the printed word that a warning must be issued about these curious spelling pronunciations.

WORD	SAY	NOT
comfort	KUMM-fort	KOMM-fort
cupboard	KUBB-'rd	KUPP-BOHRD
forehead	FORR-id, FOHR-, FAWR-	FOHR-HEDD
heroine	HERR-o-in	HERR-oyn
hiccough	HIK-up	HIK-koff
often	OFF-'n	OFF-ten
raspberry	RAZZ-berr-ee	RASP-berr-ee
said	SEDD	SAYD
says	SEZZ	SAYZ
whooping cough	HOOP-ing KOFF, KAWF	WOOP-ing KOFF
women	WIMM-in	WOH-men

The *spelling CH* so often has the sound of TCH, as in *chin,* that a common mistake is to tend to pronounce it always this way. But CH, especially in words taken from Greek, may also have the sound of K:

WORD	SAY	NOT
archives	AHR-kyvz	AHR-tchyvz
archipelago	ahr-ki-PELL-a-go	ahr-tchi-PELL-a-go
archangel	AHRK-ayn-jel	AHRTCH-ayn-jel
chasm	KAZZ-'m	TCHAZZ-'m
chimera	ky-MIRR-a, ki-	tchy-MIRR-a
chiropodist	ki-ROPP-o-dist	tchi-ROPP-o-dist
chiropractor	KY-ro-prak-tor	TCHY-ro-prak-tor
machinations	mak-i-NAY-sh'nz	mach-i-NAY-sh'nz
schizophrenic	skizz-o-FRENN-ik	———

But notice:

archbishop	ahrtch-BISH-op	ahrk-BISH-op
archdeacon	ahrtch-DEE-k'n	ahrk-DEE-k'n
schism	SIZZ'm	SKIZZ-'m

The *spelling CH,* especially in words taken from French, may also have the sound of SH:

WORD	SAY	NOT
cache	KASH	KATCH
chaise	SHAYZ, or SHEZZ	TCHAYZ
chamois	SHAM-ee	TCHAM-ee
chassis	SHASS-ee	TCHASS-ee
chic	SHEEK	TCHIK
chicanery	shi-KAYN-er-ee	tchi-KAYN-er-ee

The *spelling* G is troublesome because it has three pronunciations. The hard G of *get*, the J of *jet*, and the ZH sound as in *pleasure* may be confused in the following words:

WORD	SAY	NOT
beige	BAYZH	BAYJ
garage	ga-RAHZH	ga-RAHJ
gesture	JESS-tcher	GUESS-tcher
gesticulate	jess-TIK-yoo-layt	guess-TIK-yoo-layt
gibbet	JIB-et	GIB-et
mirage	mi-RAHZH	mi-RAHJ
regime	re-ZHEEM	re-JEEM
rouge	ROOZH	ROOJ

Reversing the Order of Sounds

If spelling is not looked at carefully enough, mispronunciations may occur because the order of certain sounds is reversed:

WORD	SAY	NOT
bronchial	BRONG-kee-al	BRONN-i-kal
cavalry	KAVV-al-ree	KAL-va-ree
irrelevant	ir-RELL-e-vant	ir-REVV-e-lant
larynx	LARR-ingks	LAHR-niks
pharynx	FARR-ingks	FAHR-niks
relevant	RELL-e-vant	REVV-e-lant

The sound R is particularly troublesome in this respect:

WORD	SAY	NOT
children	TCHILL-dren	TCHILL-dern
hundred	HUN-dred	HUN-derd
modern	MODD-ern	MODD-ren
incongruous	in-KONG-groo-us	in-KONG-ger-us
pattern	PATT-ern	PATT-ren
perspiration	pur-spir-AY-shun	press-pir-AY-shun

Added Sounds

In uneducated speech, sounds may be added to words because of their similarity to other words or because of a mistaken idea of their spelling.

WORD	SAY	NOT
across	a-KROSS	a-KROST
attack	a-TAKK	a-TAKT
attacked	a-TAKT	a-TAKK-ted
aureomycin	aw-ree-o-MY-sin	aw-ree-o-MY-o-sin
column	KOLL-um	KOLL-yum
drowned	DROWND	DROWN-ded
escape	es-KAYP	eks-KAYP
grievous	GREEV-us	GREEV-ee-us
height	HYT	HYT'TH

WORD	SAY	NOT
mischievous	MISS-tchiv-us	miss-TCHEEV-ee-us
once	WUNSS	WUNST
streptomycin	strep-to-MY-sin	strep-to-My-o-sin
wash	WAHSH, WAWSH	WAHRSH, WAWRSH
Washington	WAHSH-ing-ton, WAWSH-ing-ton	WAHRSH-ing-ton, WAWRSH-ing-ton

Sounds Left Out

Where two vowels occur together in a word, one is sometimes left out so that a syllable is lost. This sounds careless.

WORD	SAY	NOT
cruel	KROO-el	KROOL
diary	DY-a-ree	DY-ree
jewel	JOO-el	JOOL
poem	POH-em	POHM
ruin	ROO-in	ROON
violet	VY-o-let	VY-let

The mistake of leaving out a syllable may occur in other types of words:

WORD	SAY	NOT
president	PREZZ-i-dent	PREZZ-dent
probably	PROBB-a-blee	PROBB-lee
regularly	REGG-yoo-lar-lee	REGG-yu-lee
valuable	VALL-yoo-a-b'l	VALL-a-b'l

In careless speech, consonants are often left out. Be sure to say the consonants in these words:

WORD	SAY	NOT
all right	AWL RYT	AW RYT
Arctic	AHRK-tik	AHR-tik
district	DISS-trikt	DISS-trik
exactly	eg-ZAKT-lee	eg-ZAK-lee
flaccid	FLAKK-sid	FLASS-id
gentleman	JENN-tel-man	JENN-l-man
help	HELP	HEPP
hound	HOWND	HOWN
hundred	HUNN-dred	HUNN-ed
recognize	REKK-og-nyz	REKK-o-nyz
succinct	sukk-SINGT	su-SINGT
thousand	THOW-zand	THOW-zan
told	TOHLD	TOHL

Substitution of One Sound for Another

One sound is sometimes mistakenly substituted for another. This may be a foreignism or a spelling pronunciation.

WORD	SAY	NOT
average	AVV-er-ij	AVV-er-itch
because	be-KAWZ	be-KOSS, be-KAWSS
college	KOLL-ej	KOLL-itch
electricity	e-lekk-TRISS-i-tee	e'lekk-TRIZZ-i-tee
gas	GASS	GAZZ

Sound-substitutions also occur in uneducated or provincial speech. Some of the pronunciations may once have been acceptable, but are now considered archaic.

WORD	SAY	NOT
deaf	DEFF	DEEF
drama	DRAH-ma, DRAMM-a	DRAY-ma

faucet	FAW-sit	FASS-it
genuine	JENN-yoo-in	JENN-yoo-wyn
ignoramus	ig-no-RAY-mus	ig-no-RAM-us
length	LENGTH, LENGKTH	LENTH
pincers	PINN-surz	PINCH-urz
radiator	RAY-dee-ay-tor	RADD-ee-ay-tor
radio	RAY-dee-o	RADD-ee-o
rather	RATH-er, RAHTH-er	RUTH-er
rinse	RINSS	RENTCH
strength	STRENGTH, STRENGKTH	STRENTH
tremendous	tre-MENN-dus	tre-MENN-jus
wrestle	RESS-'l	RASS-'l

The letter *X* may cause confusion because it has two pronunciations, KS and GZ. In words beginning with *ex-*, which have the accent on the first syllable, the *ex* is pronounced EKS (*exodus*, EKS-o-dus). This is also the case if the accent falls on the second syllable and the second syllable begins with a consonant (*expect*, eks-PEKT). But if the second and accented syllable begins with a vowel, the sound is either EGZ or IGZ, *exalt* (egz-AWLT, igz-AWLT). Note, however:

exit	either EKS-it or EGZ-it
exile	either EKS-yl or EGZ-yl
luxury	LUKK-shu-ree
luxurious	either lukk-SHUR-i-us or lugg-ZHUR-i-us

Confusing Words with Similar Spelling

Words of different meaning but similar spelling are sometimes confused in pronunciation:

WORD AND MEANING	SAY
adjoin, to lie next to	a-JOYN
adjourn, to suspend a session	a-JURN
aural, pertaining to the hearing or the ear	AW-ral
oral, pertaining to the spoken word or the mouth	OH-ral
coral, skeleton of a sea animal	KORR-al
corral, pen for horses	ko-RAL

Word		Say
crochet, kind of needlework	kro-SHAY	
crotchet, a perverse fancy	KROTCH-et	
croquet, a lawn game	kro-KAY	
croquette, crumbed, fried minced meat	kro-KETT	
era, period of time	EE-ra, IRR-a	
err, to be mistaken	UR	
error, a mistake	ERR-or, ERR-a	
lineament, feature of the face	LINN-ee-a-ment	
liniment, liquid for sprains	LINN-i-ment	
precedence, priority in order of rank	pre-SEE-dens	
precedents, cases which serve as examples	PRESS-e-dens	
slough, a reedy or marshy pool	SLOO	
slough, n., soft muddy place; condition of degradation; v., to plod through mud	SLOW (OW as in HOW)	
slough, to cast off skin	SLUFF	
viola, a stringed instrument	ve-OH-la, vy-OH-la	
Viola	VY-o-la, VEE-o-la, ve-OH-la, vy-OH-la	

Accenting the Wrong Syllable

The accenting of certain syllables is an important feature of English pronunciation. Mistakes in placing the accent are either wrong guesses made by persons who have not yet acquired the habit of looking up pronunciations in a dictionary, or are relics of older pronunciations now too infrequently used to be considered acceptable. The list below gives both the acceptable and the unacceptable forms of words in which the accent is frequently misplaced.

WORD	SAY	NOT
acumen	a-KYOO-men	AKK-yoo-men
alias	AY-lee-as	a-LY-as
brigand	BRIG-and	bri-GAND
cabal	ka-BAL (as in *cat*)	KABB-al
cement	si-MENT	SEE-ment
Clematis	KLEMM-a-tiss	kle-MAT-iss

WORD	SAY	NOT
condolence	konn-DOH-lens	KONN-do-lens
contribute	konn-TRIBB-yoot	KONN-tri-byoot
decade	DEKK-ayd, DEKK-ad	de-KAYD
demonstrate	DEMM-on-strayt	de-MONN-strayt
disciple	di-SY-p'l	DISS-i-p'l
elixir	i-LIKK-sur	ELL-ik-sur
episcopal	e-PIS-ko-pal	ep-i-SKAH-pal
exigency	EKK-si-jen-see	ek-SIJJ-en-see
exponent	ek-SPOH-nent	EKS-poh-nent
gondola	GONN-do-la	gon-DOH-la
grimace	gri-MAYSS	GRIMM-as
horizon	ho-RY-z'n	HORR-i-zon
hyperbole	hy-PUR-bo-lee	HY-pur-bohl
incognito	in-KOGG-ni-toh	in-kogg-NEE-toh
influence	IN-floo-enss	in-FLOO-enss
integral	IN-te-gral	in-TEGG-ral
lyceum	ly-SEE-um	LY-see-um
municipal	myoo-NISS-a-p'l	myoo-ni-SIPP-'l
museum	myoo-ZEE-um	MYOO-zee-um
police	po-LEESS	POH-leess
robust	roh-BUST	ROH-bust
sepulchre	SEPP-ul-kur	se-PULL-kurr (as in *cut*)
theater	THEE-a-tur (*th* as in *thin*)	thi-YITT-ur, the-AY-tur
vagary	va-GAYR-ee	VAYG-a-ree

Notice that a root may cause a misplaced accent:

impious	IMM-pee-us	imm-PY-us
impotent	IMM-po-tent	imm-POH-tent

The four-syllable adjectives ending in *-able* (*admirable*) are frequently mispronounced. The mistaken tendency is to accent them on the second syllable, usually on the analogy of the word from which they have been formed (*admire*). These adjectives are correctly accented on the first syllable.

WORD	SAY	NOT
amicable	AMM-i-ka-b'l	a-MIKK-a-b'l
admirable	ADD-mir-a-b'l	ad-MY-ra-b'l
applicable	APP-li-ka-b'l	a-PLIKK-a-b'l
comparable	KOMM-pa-ra-b'l	komm-PAYR-a-b'l
despicable	DESS-pik-a-b'l	de-SPIKK-a-b'l

equitable	EKK-wit-a-b'l	e-KWITT-a-b'l	
formidable	FAWR-mid-a-b'l	fawr-MIDD-a-b'l	
hospitable	HOSS-pit-a-b'l	hoss-PITT-a-b'l	
lamentable	LAMM-en-ta-b'l	la-MENT-a-b'l	
preferable	PREFF-ur-a-b'l	pre-FUR-a-b'l	
reputable	REPP-yoo-ta-b'l	re-PYOO-ta-b'l	

Notice also:

indefatigable	in-de-FATT-i-ga-b'l	(do not accent the 2nd or 4th syllable)
irreparable	i-REPP-a-ra-b'l	i-re-PAYR-a-b'l
irrevocable	i-REVV-o-ka-b'l	i-re-VOH-ka-b'l

But **indisputable** may be said either as in-dis-PYOO-ta-b'l or in-DISS-pyoo-ta-b'l.

Affectations

Certain persons go out of their way to pronounce words differently from their acquaintances or from the educated persons of their part of the country. They seek out Britishisms, or poetic or archaic pronunciations and seem to put quotes around each of these whenever they say them.

Avoid such affectation. Let the pronunciations of the educated people of your region be good enough for you.

WORD	SAY	NOT
aerial	AYR-ee-al	ay-IRR-ee-al
aeroplane	AYR-o-playn	AY-e-ro-playn
again	a-GENN	a-GAYN (unless you're coastal New England)
coupon	KOO-pon	KYOO-pon
either	EE-ther	Y-ther
hearth	HAHRTH	HURTH
hygiene	HY-jeen	HY-ji-een
issue	ISH-oo	ISS-yoo
laboratory	LABB-o-ra-toh-ree	LABB-ra-tree
nature	NAYTCH-er	NAYT-yoor
neither	NEE-ther	NY-ther
rabies	RAY-beez	RAY-bi-eez
stature	STATCH-er	STATT-yoor
vase	VAYSS, VAYZ	VAHZ (British pronunciation)

Some persons who are not trying to act superior but are merely trying to be careful, try too hard, and succeed in **sounding affected.**

One instance of this is saying the ending *-ness* as if it were an accented syllable, NESS. The ending is always unaccented and should be said with an indeterminate vowel, resembling NISS.

EXAMPLE	SAY	NOT
madness	MADD-niss	MADD-ness

Another instance is saying the ending *-or* as AWR. This ending is also unaccented and should be said with an indeterminate vowel, resembling ER.

EXAMPLE	SAY	NOT
actor	AKK-ter	AKK-tawr

HELPS TOWARD BETTER PRONUNCIATION

Influence of Part of Speech on Pronunciation

Certain words are accented on the first syllable when used as nouns or adjectives, on the second when used as verbs.

EXAMPLES	NOUN OR ADJ.	VERB
absent	ABB-sent	ab-SENT
addict	ADD-ikt	a-DIKT
annex	ANN-eks	a-NEKS
perfect	PUR-fekt	per-FEKT

Other words which shift accent in this way are:

collect	export	project
combat	import	rebel
combine	imprint	record
compound	incense	reject
conduct	increase	subject
contract	permit	survey
convert	prefix	suspect
desert	present	transfer
digest	produce	transport
escort	progress	

Notice, however:

WORD	NOUN OR ADJ.	VERB
attribute	ATT-ri-byoot	a-TRIBB-yoot
consummate	kon-SUMM-it	KONN-su-mayt
perfume	PUR-fyoom, per-FYOOM	per-FYOOM
refuse	REFF-yooss	re-FYOOZ

The word *adept* is pronounced ADD-ept when used as a noun, a-DEPT when used as an adjective.

The word *compact* is pronounced KOMM-pakt when used as a noun, kom-PAKT when used as a verb, and either KOMM-pakt or kom-PAKT when used as an adjective.

The word *cleanly* is pronounced KLENN-lee when used as an adjective, KLEEN-lee when used as an adverb.

When certain words ending in -*ate* are used as verbs, this last syllable is pronounced AYT. But when they are used as adjectives or nouns, the final vowel is indeterminate in quality and the syllable resembles -IT.

EXAMPLES	NOUN OR ADJ.	VERB
advocate	ADD-vo-kit	ADD-vo-kayt
aggregate	AGG-re-git	AGG-re-gayt

Other words which shift pronunciation in this way are:

alternate	deliberate	intimate
appropriate	designate	moderate
approximate	desolate	predicate
associate	duplicate	separate
degenerate	estimate	
delegate	graduate	

Note, however, that *prostrate* is pronounced PROSS-trayt both as verb and as adjective.

Words We Read but Seldom Say

Writing tends to be formal, to use learned (LURN-ed) words. In talking, we try for informality, directness, simplicity.

Therefore, there are many words which we read and know the meaning of, but which we seldom hear and seldom say. And when we do have to say them, as when we read aloud to our family or friends from a newspaper or magazine, we are frequently at a loss as to how to pronounce them.

The list below contains a sampling of such words. Read them. Say them out loud. Memorize their pronunciation. Check them in your dictionary. Make a habit of looking up the pronunciation of other "hard" words when you come across them.

Only a few mispronunciations are given below, for the simple reason that the words are not said often enough to acquire any common mispronunciations.

WORD AND MEANING	PRONOUNCED
aborigines, primitive inhabitants	ab-o-RIJ-i-neez
abstemious, sparing in diet	ab-STEE-mee-us
aggrandizement, enlargement in size or power	a-GRANN-diz-ment
bestial, brutal, inhuman	BESS-tchel, BEST-yal
congeries, collection of particles in a mass	kon-JIRR-eez, kon-JIRR-i-eez
Deity, the; God	DEE-i-tee (not DAY-i-tee)
demise, death	di-MYZ
demoniacal, possessed by an evil spirit	dee-mo-NY-a-kal
egregious, remarkably flagrant: *an egregious lie*	e-GREE-jus, e-GREE-ji-us
epitome, a summary	e-PITT-o-mee (not EPP-i-tohm)
harbinger, a forerunner	HAHR-bin-jer
heinous, hateful, odious	HAY-nus
inveigle, to win over by guile	in-VEE-g'l, in-VAY-g'l
lugubrious, ridiculously mournful	loo-GYOO-bri-us
malinger, to feign sickness to avoid work	ma-LING-ger
phlegmatic, not easily excited	flegg-MATT-ik
promulgate, to proclaim formally	pro-MULL-gayt

recluse, a person who lives in seclusion	re-KLOOSS, REKK-looss	
spontaneity, action proceeding from an inner impulse	spon-ta-NEE-i-tee (not NAY-i-tee)	
squalor, foulness	SKWOLL-or	
unguent, a salve, or ointment	UNG-gwent	
zealot, one showing excess of zeal	ZELL-ot	

Choice of Pronunciation

Sometimes persons dispute about the pronunciation of a word, not realizing that two (or even more) pronunciations of that word are equally acceptable. The unabridged dictionaries carry a special section devoted to such words.

Below is a list of fairly common words for which a choice of pronunciation is allowed. Of the pronunciations given, plan to use the one you hear most frequently among your friends or in your part of the country. Follow the same practice when you find two or more pronunciations given in a dictionary.

WORD	SAY EITHER	OR
abdomen	ABB-do-men	ab-DOH-men
adult	a-DULT	ADD-ult
advertisement	ad-VUR-tiss-ment	ad-ver-TYZ-ment
almond	AMM-ond	AH-mond
alternate, n., adj.	AWL-ter-nit AL-ter-nit	awl-TUR-nit al-TUR-nit
alternate, v.	AWL-ter-nayt	AL-ter-nayt
amenable	a-MEE-na-b'l	a-MEN-a-b'l
apparatus	app-a-RAY-tus	app-a-RATT-us
aspirant	a-SPYR-ant	ASS-pi-rant
banal	BAY-nal, BANN-al	ba-NAL, ba-NAHL
betroth	be-TROTH	be-TROHTH
betrothal	be-TROTH-al	be-TROH-thal
brusque	BRUSK	BRUUSK (as in *look*)
calliope (steam organ)	KAL-ee-ohp	ka-LY-o-pee
cerebral	SERR-e-bral	se-REE-bral
chastisement	TCHASS-tiz-ment	tchass-TYZ-ment
chauffeur	SHOW-fer	sho-FUR
coadjutor	koh-a-JOO-tor	ko-AJJ-u-tor
combatant	KOMM-ba-tant	kom-BATT-ant
conduit	KONN-dit	KONN-doo-it

WORD	SAY EITHER	OR
contractor	KONN-trak-tor	kon-TRAK-tor
dais	DAY-iss	DAYSS
decadent	de-KAY-dent	DEKK-a-dent
defect	di-FEKT	DEE-fekt
detail, n.	di-TAYL	DEE-tayl
but detail, v.	*only* di-TAYL	
diocesan	dy-OSS-e-san	dy-o-SEE-san
exquisite	EKS-kwizz-it	(for special emphasis eks-KWIZZ-it)
extant	EKS-tant	eks-TANT
extraordinary	ek-STRAWR-di-nerr-ee	eks-tra-AWR-di-nerr-ee
finance	fi-NANS	FY-nans
financier	finn-an-SEER	fy-nan-SEER
gala	GAYL-la	GAL-a
gladiolus	gladd-i-OH-lus (the plant)	gla-DY-o-lus (the genus)
grovel	GRUVV-'l	GROVV-'l
harass	HAR-is (as in *cat*)	ha-RASS
hovel	HUVV-'l	HOVV-'l
illustrate	ILL-u-strayt	i-LUSS-trayt
indissolubly	in-DISS-o-lyoo-blee	in-di-SOLL-yoo-blee
inquiry	in-KWYR-ee	IN-kwi-ree
isolate	Y-so-layt	ISS-olayt
jocund	JOKK-und	JOH-kund
obligatory	o-BLIGG-a-toh-ree	OBB-li-ga-toh-ree
patronize	PAY-tro-nyz	PATT-ron-yz
penalize	PEE-na-lyz	PENN-a-lyz
persist	pur-SIST	pur-ZIST
pianist	pi-ANN-ist	PEE-a-nist
quinine	KWY-nyn	kwi-NEEN
ration	RASH-on	RAY-shon
reservoir	REZZ-er-vawr	REZZ-er-vwahr
resource	re-SOHRS	REE-sohrs
route	ROOT	ROWT (as in *how*)
sacrilegious	sak-ri-LIJJ-us	sakk-ri-LEE-jus
vaudeville	VOHD-vill	VAW-di-vill
version	VURR-zhon	VURR-shon

Note that *provost* and *oblique* are pronounced PROVV-ost and o-BLEEK in civilian life, proh-VOH and o-BLYK in military life. *Carbine* is pronounced both KAHR-byn and KAHR-been.

Words ending in *-ile* present no definite pattern with regard to pronunciation, some taking -ILL, some -YL (as in *file*), and some either -ILL or -YL.

A choice of either -ILL or -YL is allowed in: **infantile, juvenile, senile, versatile.**

-ILL is preferred by Americans in: **agile, docile, futile, hostile, textile,** and **virile** (VIRR-ill or VY-ril). Britishers use -YL for these words.

But **sterile** takes only -ILL, and **exile, gentile** and **profile** take only -YL.

FOREIGN WORDS AND PHRASES

Latin Words and Phrases

The following words and phrases taken from Latin are fairly often encountered in English. They are heard in business, law, logic, politics, the arts, and in conversation generally.

A brief definition accompanies each entry.

WORD AND MEANING	SAY
a fortiori; with the greater force, said of one conclusion as compared with another	AY fawr-shi-AW-ry
ad infinitum; without limit	ADD in-fi-NY-tum
ad libitum (ad lib); as one wishes	ADD LIBB-i-tum
alma mater; fostering mother; hence, one's school	AHL-ma MAH-ter, AL-ma MAY-ter
alumnus, /i, /a, /ae; graduate of a school	masc. a-LUMM-nus, pl. -ny; fem. -na, pl. -nee
anno Domini; in the year of the Christian era	ANN-oh DOMM-i-nee
a posteriori; known afterwards; hence, through experience	AY poss-tirr-i-OH-ree
a priori; known beforehand; hence, through reasoning	AY pri-OH-ry, pry-OH-ry; AH pri-OH-ree
bona fide; in good faith	BOH-na FY-de; as adj., BOH-na FYD, BONN-a
carpe diem; enjoy the day	KAHR-pe DY-em
corpus delicti; in a murder case, the actual death of the one alleged to have been murdered	KAWR-pus di-LIKK-ty
data; things given, esp. facts on which an inference is based	DAY-ta, DATT-a
de facto; actually, in fact	DEE FAKK-toh
de jure; by right or lawful title	DEE JOO-ree
dramatis personae; characters in a drama	DRAMM-a-tiss pur-SOH-nee
ex cathedra; by virtue of one's office	EKS ka-THEE-dra
ex officio; by virtue of an office	EKS o-FISH-i-oh
ex post facto; done afterwards but retroactive	EKS POHST FAKK-toh
extempore; without preparation	eks-TEMM-po-ree
finis; end	FY-niss
gratis; for nothing	GRAY-tiss, GRATT-iss
habeas corpus; a writ to bring a person before a court	HAY-be-us KAWR-pus
imprimatur; license to publish a book	imm-pri-MAY-tur, -pry—
in absentia; in absence	IN abb-SENN-she-a
in extremis; near death	IN eks-TREE-miss
in toto; entirely	IN TOH-toh
non sequitur; a conclusion which does not follow from the premises	NONN SEKK-wi-tur, NAHN-
obiter dictum, -a; incidental remark or observation	OBB-i-ter DIKK-tum
per diem; by the day	PUR DY-em
persona non grata; an unacceptable person	pur-SOH-na NONN (NAHN) GRAY-ta
prima facie; at first view	PRY-ma FAY-shi-ee, FAY-shi
pro rata; according to share	PROH RAY-ta, RAH-ta
pro tempore (pro tem); for the time being	PROH TEMM-po-ree
quasi; as if, seeming	KWAY-sy, KWAH-see
re; with reference to	REE
sine die; without naming a day to meet again	SY-ni DY-ee

status; state of a person or affairs	STAY-tus, STATT-us
status quo; the state existing	STAY-tus KWOH, STATT-us
stratum, -a; a layer or level	STRAY-tum, STRATT-um, plur. -ta
subpoena; a writ commanding appearance in court	su-PEE-na, sub-
ultimatum; a final proposition	ull-ti-MAY-tum
verbatim; word for word	vur-BAY-tum
via; by way of	VY-a, VEE-a
viva voce; orally	VY-va VOH-see
vox populi; voice of the people	VOKKS POPP-yoo-ly

French Words and Phrases

The French words and phrases in the lists below occur fairly frequently in English. They have been grouped in several categories, but of course they may be used in other fields.

When we say these words and phrases we usually tend only to approximate the French pronunciation, to give them a slightly French flavor, as it were. Sometimes we Anglicize them entirely, saying them as if they were native words.

When an N is italicized below as in *en* (AHN), it means that the preceding vowel is nasalized (with the soft palate dropped slightly and the tone allowed to resonate in the nose) while the N itself is silent.

French syllables are more evenly stressed than English syllables, with a slight stress on the last syllable of the word or phrase. This is frequently carried over into English, as in **à la carte** (ah la KAHRT).

Food and Restaurant Words

WORD AND MEANING	SAY
à la carte; dish by dish, with a stated price for each	ah la KAHRT
à la mode; 1. dessert served with ice cream, 2. stewed or braised with vegetables and served with gravy, 3. fashionable	ah la MOHD, AL a mohd
cuisine; style of cooking	kwe-ZEEN
entrée; 1. main course of a meal, 2. the dish before the main course, 3. right of entry	AHN-tray
filet mignon; round fillet of beef	fee-lay-mee-NYAWN, fe-LAY MEEN-yonn
garçon; waiter, boy	gahr-SAWN
gourmand; a lover of good eating	GOOR-mand, goor-MAHN
gourmet; one who shows taste in appreciating good food	GOOR-may, goor-MAY
hors-d'oeuvre; appetizer	AWR DU(R)VR (like an UR without R)
menu; bill of fare	MENN-yoo, MAY-nyoo
pièce de résistance; main dish	PYESS de-ray-zees-TAHNSS
table d'hôte; meal for which one pays a fixed price	TAH-b'l DOHT, TABB-'l

Military Words

WORD AND MEANING	SAY
aide de camp; officer-assistant to a general	AYD de KAMP, EDD-de-KAHN
camouflage; disguise of a camp, and so any disguise expedient	KAMM-o-flahzh (zh, like *s* in plea*s*ure)
corps; body of persons under common direction	KOHR (not KAWRPSS) plur. KOHRZ
coup de grâce; a finishing stroke	KOO de GRAHSS
hors de combat; disabled and so out of the combat	awr de kawn-BA (part-way between c*a*t and c*a*lm)

Words from the Arts

WORD AND MEANING	SAY
bas-relief; sculpture in low relief	bah re-LEEF, BAH re-leef, BASS (as in c*a*t)
baton; conductor's stick, staff of office	ba-TONN, BATT-on
belles-lettres; aesthetic, rather than informational, literature	bell LETT'r
connoisseur; one competent as a critic of art	konn-i-SUR
façade; face of a building, front of anything	fa-SAHD
nom de plume; pen name	NOMM de ploom
protégé; one under protection of another	PROH-te-zhay
tour de force; feat of strength or skill	toor de FAWRSS

Political Words and Phrases

WORD AND MEANING	SAY
bourgeoisie; members of the middle class	boor-zhwah-ZEE
cause célèbre; legal case of great interest	kohz se-LEBB'r
detente; a relaxation of tensions (as between nations)	day-TAH*N*T
entente cordiale; cordial understanding between two governments	ah*n*-TAH*N*T kawr-DYAL
laissez faire; non-interference	LESS-ay FAYR

Social and General Words

WORD AND MEANING	SAY
au revoir; goodby till we meet again	oh re-VWAHR
beau geste; ingratiating act or gesture	boh ZHEST
bête noire; bugbear	bett NWAHR, bayt
billet doux; love letter	BILL-i doo, BILL-ay, plur. dooz
bon vivant; lover of good living	baw*n* vee-VAH*N*
carte blanche; unconditional power	KAHRT BLAHNSH
château; 1. castle, 2. large country house	sha-TOH

WORD AND MEANING	SAY
cortège; 1. procession, 2. train of attendants	kawr-TEZH, -TAYZH
crèche; representation of the figures at Bethlehem	KRESH, KRAYSH
cul-de-sac; a blind alley or deadlock	KULL de sakk (or *u* as in p*u*ll)
début; entrance on a career or into society	DAY-byoo, de-BYOO
débutante; one making a debut	debb-yoo-TAHNT, DEBB-yoo-tant
{**deshabille;** loose or careless style	dezz-a-BEEL
}**dishabille;** of dress	diss-a-BEEL
élite; the choice part, as of a group	i-LEET, ay-LEET
enfant terrible; child whose remarks cause embarrassment	ah*n*-fah*n* te-REEB'l
en route; on the way	ahn ROOT
faux pas; false step; offense against social convention	foh PAH, plur. PAHZ
gauche; awkward	GOHSH
gendarme; policeman	ZHAHN-dahrm
joie de vivre; keen enjoyment of life	zhwa de VEE'vr (*a* between c*a*t and c*a*lm)
loge; box in a theatre	LOHZH
mal-de-mer; seasickness	mal de MERR
qui vive, on the; on the alert	kee VEEV
sang-froid; coolness in any circumstance	sah*n* FRWA
savoir faire; social ease and grace	SAVV-wahr FAYR
suite; 1. set, 2. retinue, 3. instrumental composition	SWEET
tête-à-tête; conversation for two alone	tett a TETT, tayt a TAYT
vis-a-vis; face to face	vee-za-VEE

German Words and Phrases

A few German words have gained acceptance in English speech.

WORD AND MEANING	SAY
auf Wiedersehen; till we meet again	owff VEE-der-ZAYN
ersatz; substitute	err-ZAHTSS
Gesundheit; to your health	ge-ZUUNT-hyt (UU as in p*u*t)

WORD AND MEANING	SAY
Lebensraum; territory desired by a nation for expansion	LAY-benss-ROWM (OW as in h*ow*)
leitmotif; theme associated with a person or idea	LYT-moh-teef
Reichstag; Germ. legislative assembly	RYKS-tahg
verboten; forbidden	fer-BOH-ten
wanderlust; strong impulse to wander	WONN-der-lust, VAHN-der-lust
Weltanschauung; world-view	VELT AHN-show-ung (ow as in h*ow*)
Weltschmerz; sadness from a pessimistic world-view	VELT-shmerrts
Zeitgeist; spirit of the times	TSYT-gyst

Italian Words

A great many Italian words are used by musicians and artists. Below are a few words which present special pronunciation problems:

WORD AND MEANING	SAY
adagio; slowly	a-DAH-joh, -zhoh (*zh* like *s* in pleasure)
concerto; composition for one or several instruments and orchestra	kon-TCHERR-toh
crescendo; gradual increase in volume	kre-SHENN-doh
Fascisti; Ital. anti-socialism, anti-democracy followers of Mussolini	fa-SHISS-tee, -SHEESS-
piazza; veranda	pi-AZZ-a, Brit. pi-ATT-sa
pizzicato; plucked	pitt-si-KAH-toh
vivace; lively	vee-VAH-tchee

NAMES OF PERSONS AND PLACES

Names of Persons

The names of persons are often a troublesome problem in pronunciation. For family names, the family itself decides how its name is to be pronounced.

The following lists contain examples of choices in the pronunciation of names, or of common mispronunciations.

Family Names

NAME	USUALLY PRONOUNCED
Beauchamp	BEE-tcham (not BOH-shah*n*)
Knopf	KNOPPF (not NOPPF)
MacLeod	ma-KLOWD (as in *cloud*)
McLean	ma-KLAYN (not mak-LEEN)
Monroe	munn-ROH (not MONN-roh)
Pierce	PIRRSS or PURRSS
Roosevelt	ROHZ-e-velt, or ROHZ-velt (not ROOZ-e-velt)
Van Wyck	vann WYK (not vann WIKK)
Xavier	ZAY-vi-er (not ekk-ZAY-vi-er)

Nationalities

Arab	AR-ab (not AY-rab)
Celtic	SELL-tik or KELL-tik
Czech	TCHEKK
Maori	MAH-o-ree, MOW-ree (ow as in h*ow*) MAH-ree
Italian	i-TAL-yan (not Y-TAL-yan)

Note also:

Magi	MAY-jy (not MAGG-y)

Composers

Bartok	BAHR-tokk, -tohk
Beethoven	BAY-toh-ven
Berlioz	BERR-li-ohz
Chopin	SHOH-pann, shoh-PA*NN*
Debussy	de-BYOO-see, or Fr. de-bu-SEE (u as a lip-rounded EE)
de Falla	de FAHL-ya
Dvorak	DVAWR-zhakk, -zhahk
Haydn	HY-d'n
Purcell	PUR-sel (not pur-SELL)
Saint-Saëns	sa*n* SAH*N*S
Shostakovitch	shoss-tah-KOH-vitch
Villa-Lobos	VEE-lah LAW-bawss
Wagner	VAHG-ner

Authors

Balzac	BAL-zakk or BAWL-zakk
Boccaccio	boh-KAH-tchi-o

Cellini	tche-LEE-nee
Cervantes	ser-VANN-teez, ser-VAHN-tayss
Dostoevsky	dawss-to-YEFF-skee
Dumas	DYOO-mah, DOO-mah
Goethe	GOE-tuh (for OE, lips rounded as for OH, while trying to say AY), GU(R)-tuh
Maeterlinck	MAY-ter-lingk
Maugham	MAWM
Pepys	PEEPS, PEPS, PEP-iss
Yeats	YAYTS

Characters

Adonis	a-DOH-niss, a-DONN-iss
Aeschylus	ESS-ki-lus, Brit. EES-
Don Juan	donn JOO-an, dahn; don HWAHN
Don Quixote	donn KWIKK-sit, don kee-Ho-tay
Odysseus	oh-DISS-yoos, oh-DISS-i-us
Oedipus	EDD-i-pus, EE-di-pus

American Place Names

The pronunciation of American place names is usually determined by the locality itself. Interesting differences occur, and the pronunciations of one part of the country often surprises those living elsewhere. The following list contains examples of some of the more outstanding pronunciations, and also compares American with British examples. (In the *Foreign Place Names* list, compare the foreign and native pronunciations for **Cairo, Delhi, Lima.**)

NAME	SAY
Albuquerque	AL-bu-kurr-kee
Arkansas (the state)	AHR-kan-saw
Arkansas River	ahr-KANN-zas
Boise	BOY-zee, BOY-see
Butte	BYOOT
Cheyenne	shy-ENN
Chicago	shi-KAW-goh, -KAH- (not tchi-KAH-goh)
Chisholm	TCHIZZ-um
Des Moines	de MOYN
Derby	DUR-bee
(compare with *British*)	DAHR-bee

NAME	SAY
Greenwich Village, N.Y.	GRENN-itch
(compare with *Greenwich, Eng.*)	GRIN-ij, GRENN-itch
Houston, Tex.	HYOO-ston
Houston St., N.Y.C.	HOW-ston
Iowa	Y-o-way (locally); Y-o-wa
Los Angeles	loss ANG-ge-les, ANN-je-les, -leez
Missouri	mi-ZOOR-i, -ee, -a
Montana	monn-TANN-a, -TAH-na
Pierre, South Dakota	PEER
St. Louis	saynt LOO-iss, LOO-ee
Schuyler	SKY-ler
Schuylkill	SKOOL-kill
Spokane	spo-KANN
Spuyten Duyvil	SPY-ten DY-vil
Terre Haute	TERR-e HOHT
Thames, U.S.	THAYMZ, TAYMZ, TEMMZ
(compare with *British*)	TEMMZ

Foreign Place Names

Foreign place names fall into two categories with regard to their pronunciation in English:

The names of the larger, better-known cities and towns are completely Anglicized. We say mi-LANN or MILL-an for Milan, as if it were a native word, and with no thought of the fact that Italians call the place mee-LAH-noh.

For the less well-known places, we tend to approximate the foreign pronunciation, partially Anglicizing it, and sometimes keeping only one element of the original pronunciation. *Nice* is said NEESS.

Choices are possible for fairly well-known places. Difficulties in pronunciation occur when, for some reason, places formerly obscure suddenly become well-known. The following list contains some interesting examples of the pronunciation of foreign place names.

NOTE: You may use the foreign pronunciation of a place name if you wish, but do so only if your command of the foreign language is good and if you find that your friends and acquaintances do not raise their eyebrows at such attempts. Of course, if you are going abroad, learn the foreign pronunciation of place names while you are studying the language.

NAME	SAY
Aix-la-Chapelle	EKKS lah-shah-PELL
Aachen (Germ. name of above)	AH-ken
Bayreuth	BY-royt
Buenos Aires	BWAY-nos Y-rizz, BOH-nos AYR-eez
Caen (compare with *Cannes*)	KAHN (nasalized AH)
Cairo, Egypt	KY-roh
(compare with *Cairo, Ill.*) KAYR-oh	
Calais	KAL-ay, KAL-is, ka-LAY
Cannes	KANN, KANNZ
Caribbean	kar-i-BEE-an, ka-RIB-ee-an
Delhi, India	DELL-ee
(compare with *Delhi, U.S.*) Dell-hy	

NAME	SAY
Guadalajara	gwah-dah-lah-HAH-rah
Himalaya	he-MAHL-ya, him-a-LAY-a
Hiroshima	hir-o-SHEE-ma
Kiev	KEE-eff
Lima, Peru	LEE-ma
(compare with *Lima, Ohio*) LY-ma	
Lourdes	LOORD
Lyons	LY-onz, lee-AWN
Madras	ma-DRASS, ma-DRAHSS
Marseilles	mahr-SAY, older, -SAYLZ
Milan	mi-LANN, MILL-an
Montevideo	MONN-te-vi-DAY-oh
(compare with *Montevideo, Minn.*) MONN-te-VIDD-i-oh	
Moscow	MOSS-kow, MOSS-koh
Nice	NEESS
Peiping	BAY-PING, formerly PEE-PING
Prague	PRAHG, older, PRAYG
Rheims	REEMZ
Rio de Janeiro	REE-oh de zha-NAYR-oh
Transvaal	trans-VAHL, tranz-
Trieste	tre-EST
Versailles	vur-SAYLZ, vayr-SY
Ypres	EE-pr

SUPPLEMENT II

BUILDING A VOCABULARY

THE IMPORTANCE OF A GOOD VO-CABULARY. In Goethe's *Faust*, Mephistopheles gives this advice to a student:

> To words hold fast!
> Then the safest gate securely pass'd.
> You'll reach the halls of certainty at last.

At least this once we ought to listen to the Devil's counsel. Without in any way trying to raise the devil, psychologists have reached the same conclusions about vocabulary. Research carried out at such institutions as Stanford University and Dr. Johnson O'Connor's Human Engineering Laboratory has verified that **size** and **accuracy** of vocabulary provide two of the most reliable guides to a man's **general ability** and, consequently, to his **potential for success.** Guided by these findings, businessmen and industrialists, before hiring would-be young executives, often test their vocabularies as well as their special knowledge. Federal, state, and municipal agencies also commonly test vocabulary as part of their examinations for various posts. Likewise, schools and colleges have discovered that good vocabulary and good work are closely related. For all of this, we are giving the devil his due.

To just how many words do men hold fast? All answers have been debated. Estimates of the average vocabulary range from 4,000 words to 12,000. Those who read extensively may, however, have **recognition vocabularies** exceeding 50,000 words. None debate this fact: whatever the number of words in a man's vo-cabulary, he can easily add to it—and benefit from the addition. Before studying the steps by which vocabulary can be improved, it will be useful to understand the differences between the kinds of vocabularies.

The **speaking** vocabulary: most limited of the vocabularies, it consists of the words used in conversation.

The cat is a self-centered animal, thinking only of itself, almost never of the world about it.

The **writing** vocabulary: more extensive than the *speaking* vocabulary, it consists of the words used in conversation and, if the writer has a wide reading background, many thousands more.

The cat is an *egocentric* creature, *tranquil* in its *self-assurance, oblivious* of the world about it.

The **reading** vocabulary: larger than either the *speaking* or *writing* vocabularies (both of which it includes), it contains words which the reader can define when he sees them, even though he neither speaks nor writes them.

The cat understands *pure being*, which is all we need to know and which it takes us a lifetime to learn. It is both *subject* and *object*. It is its own *outlet* and its own *material*. . . . The cat has a complete *subjective unity*. Being its own *centre*, it *radiates* electricity in all directions. It is *magnetic* and *impervious*. (Van Vechten, *Peter Whiffle*)

The **recognition** vocabulary: largest of the vocabularies, it contains, in addition to the other three, those words which one has seen or heard previously, but cannot clearly define. He may recognize them in context (how they are used in the sentence), but he lacks assurance about their actual meaning.

> When you notice a cat in *profound* meditation,
>   The reason, I tell you, is always the same:
> His mind is engaged in a *rapt* contemplation
>   Of the thought, of the thought, of the thought
>   of his name:
>   His *ineffable effable*
>   Effanineffable
> Deep and *inscrutable singular* Name.
>   (T. S. Eliot, *The Naming of Cats**)

The *erudite partisan* of cats understands that on the rare occasions when *felines* gather, they do so in a *"clowder"* and kittens in a *"kendle."*
(adapted from a letter to London *Times*)

Thus, anyone who intends to improve his vocabulary must learn how to transfer into his speaking and writing vocabularies, appropriate words from his reading and recognition vocabularies. To effect the transfer involves work, but the reward is proportionate to the effort.

FOR PRACTICE: The following sentences have been selected from newspapers, speeches, magazines, books, and the like. How many of the italicized words can you define or provide a synonym for?

Next to each word, indicate to which of your four vocabularies (**speaking, writing, reading, recognition**) it belongs. Then note at the end of the exercise the sources from which the material was taken. Evaluate your own vocabulary.

1. Television is here with us, *clamoring* for understanding and wise application.
2. Although Italian wines of honorable *lineage* are relatively available, wine-drinkers know little about them beyond the *ubiquitous Chianti.*
3. Those days were gone, the old brave innocent *tumultuous eupeptic tomorrowless* days.
4. Study of *scriptual* teachings, *unencumbered* by *ecclesiastical dogma*, may help to determine a *criterion* of convincing faith.
5. That *subtle* something which *effuses* behind the *whirl* of *animation*, a happy and joyous public spirit, as *distinguish'd* from a *sluggish* and *saturnine* one.

SOURCES:

1. Speaker at Town Meeting of the Air.
2. Article on wines in New York *Times Magazine.*
3. William Faulkner, *Requiem for a Nun.*
4. Letter to member of radio panel.
5. Walt Whitman, *Specimen Days.*

METHODS OF BUILDING VOCABULARY.

Many roads lead to a strong vocabulary and in this section we will map several of them, first indicating some well-paved routes and some dangerous soft shoulders.

Make your study of words a **passionate pursuit,** not a **painful prowl.** When you see *denim* advertised as one of the more popular fabrics for summer wear, do you wonder why it goes by that name? If you turn eagerly to the dictionary to discover the answer, you have an affection for words that will inevitably lead to a better vocabulary.

But if, when you come upon a sentence like this:

How can the party leaders predict victory when most of the electorate are *Mugwumps?*

you pass on in ignorance to the next sentence or grudgingly look up *Mugwump* in the diction-

---

* From *Old Possum's Book of Practical Cats*, copyright 1939, by T. S. Eliot. Reprinted by permission of Harcourt, Brace and Company, Inc.

ary, you are not even on a painful prowl—you are in **ignoble ignorance.**

Learn words that you intend to use in speaking, writing, and reading. **Don't try to learn mere lists of words.**

A Poor Method:

ephemeral .... short-lived
acrimonious .... bitter
ubiquitous .... omnipresent
clandestine .... secret
obdurate .... stubborn

Lists provide ineffectual study aids because:

They fail to tell whether the word is suitable for speaking, writing, or reading (since they give no reference to where or how the word was used).

They become too long and cannot easily be memorized.

They mistake **quantity** as the purpose of vocabulary building: **quality** (usefulness, relevance) is quite as important.

An Effective Method:

1. Enter in a small notebook or on 3 × 5 index cards only those words you want to use. Discuss only one word on a page or card.

2. List the following information from the dictionary:

a. Meanings of the word.

b. Spelling, pronunciation, syllabication, part of speech.

c. Origin (etymology), roots.

d. Use as other part of speech.

e. Synonyms, antonyms.

NOTE: Reread the passage about the dictionary in Section 5: Spelling.

3. Copy out the sentence in which you found the word. Leave space for other sentences you may come upon.

4. Jot down examples of how you have used the word in speaking or writing.

5. Keep your notebook or pack of cards handy, and study it daily. Find occasions where you can use the word in speaking and writing. (See Below)

	PART OF
	SYLLABICATION SPEECH
word	EPHEMERAL (i fem′ar al), e-phem-er-al, adjective
pronunciation	
origin	Greek: *ephemeron*, of or for only one day
meaning	Defin.—lasting but a short time, short-lived, transitory
other uses	*ephemera*—noun; *ephemerally*—adverb
synonym, antonym	Synonyms: *fleeting, evanescent, transient* Antonyms: *permanent, lasting, eternal*
how it is used	"All is *ephemeral*—fame and the famous as well." (Marcus Aurelius, *Meditations*)
space for other examples	
Student's use of	We waste too much time fretting about *ephemeral* things like taxes and the weather. We ought to pay more heed to lasting matters. (Letter to Ed Smith)

USING THE FAMILY OF TONGUES. The word *mother* has cognates (words related in origin) in many languages:

mutter—German   meter—Greek
moeder—Danish   madre—Spanish
modhir—Icelandic   mère—French
mater—Latin

After many centuries of examining interrelationships of this kind, scholars have recently discovered that men living in countries ranging from Central Asia to Western Europe speak languages derived from a parent or source language whose origin dates back about 4000 years. This parent language is commonly known as Indo-European and gave rise to the following languages:

Eastern

Sanskrit (now dead); neo-Sanskrit languages of India: Hindi, Bengali, etc.
Indo-Iranian: Persian
Armenian

Western

Celtic: Irish, Scottish, Welsh, Breton, Cornish
Italic: Latin (and other dialects like Umbrian, Etruscan); Modern Romance languages: Italian, French, Spanish, Portuguese
Hellenic: Greek
Baltic:
    EAST: Russian, Ukrainian
    WEST: Polish, Czech, Slovene
Teutonic: ENGLISH, Dutch, German, Scandinavian

Modern English passed through several stages before becoming what it is today:

Old English (Anglo-Saxon): 450 A.D.—1100 A.D.

Typical Anglo-Saxon contributions:

ARTICLES: *the, a, an*
PRONOUNS: *that, which*
PREPOSITIONS: *in, for, to, from, without*
CONJUNCTIONS: *and, but*
VERBS: *are, have, could, sit, see, run, send*
NOUNS: *mother, father, wife, husband, house, door, bed*

NOTE: Many Latin words survived from the earlier period of Roman occupation, and yet more were added when Roman missionaries began to arrive in the sixth century. About these words, more will be said later.

A Danish invasion in the eighth century added yet more monosyllabic words to the English vocabulary: *leg, sky, skin, window,* and the pronoun *they.*

Middle English: 1100-1500

The Norman Conquest in 1066 introduced the French language to England. French has since that time deeply influenced English vocabulary, particularly words about food, clothing, law, government, and the like:

mauve	felony	débris	bagatelle
adroit	grimace	intrigue	grotesque
clique	ingénue	ennui	dénouement
svelte	chauvinism	renaissance	silhouette
cliché	detour	genre	puissant

Modern English: 1500-present

Early Modern English: 16th–17th centuries
Later Modern English: 18th–19th centuries
Contemporary English: Since 1900

From 1500 forward, as commerce increased, and England's contacts with the continent and the East grew, the vocabulary of the English language expanded tremendously. The following list merely suggests some of the borrowings which have entered our vocabulary from foreign sources.

Increasingly, Americans have realized that they live, not as a single group of people separated from the rest of the world by two oceans, but as one among a great family of nations. Not at all strange, then, is the fact that

SOME ENGLISH BORROWINGS FROM FOREIGN COUNTRIES (Latin and Greek will be taken separately)

Italy	Spain	Mexico	Germany	Russia	Hungary	Netherlands
incognito	renegade	lasso	kindergarten	vodka	goulash	skipper
salvo	corral	ranch	strafe	czar	vampire	schooner
gusto	peccadillo	mesa	blitzkrieg	sable	tokay	yacht
confetti	flotilla	canyon	waltz	polka	hussar	sloop
vendetta	Negro	coyote		steppe		dock
balcony	mosquito	tomato				hull
gondola	tornado					
ditto						
bandit						
contraband						

Africa	Persia	Arabia	Sanskrit	Hebrew	Turkey	Egypt
oasis	pajama	alcohol	indigo	amen	angora	gypsy
tangerine	chess	algebra	chintz	seraph	fez	gum
gorilla	jackal	coffee	ginger	jubilee	ottoman	paper
chimpanzee	bazaar	nadir		balsam	horde	
canary	divan	zenith		Sabbath		
		ginger		cherub		
		garbage				
		cipher				

British Indian	American Indian	Japan	China	Malaya	Polynesia	Australia
polo	tomahawk	kimono	tea	ketchup	tattoo	kangaroo
coolie	wigwam	geisha	chop suey	gingham	taboo	boomerang
rupee	skunk	jinrikisha	joss	caddy		
khaki	succotash	jujitsu	sampan	gong		
curry	tobacco		soy	junk		

language too knows no boundaries, that English as known and spoken today is a composite of many foreign tongues. If, therefore, you build vocabulary from your knowledge of words borrowed from these foreign tongues, you can prove even better to yourself and to those about you that no man is alone.

Practice Exercise

Part 1. Make a list of words borrowed from the Italian for the following subjects:

MUSIC   PAINTING   LITERATURE
EXAMPLE: *solo   chiaroscuro   sonnet*

Part 2. One word has been omitted from each of the following sentences. From the list of foreign borrowings below, select the appropriate word to complete each sentence. Check the meaning and pronunciation of each word in your dictionary.

a. Surely not for this, merely whistling at the passing parade, a trifle, a ——, not for this can you hang me.

b. Blindly, zealously patriotic, ignoring his own safety, Corporal Essex, a —— to the end, gave his life for Zanzibar.

c. Wedgwood china is famed for the delicate —— patterns which adorn it.

d. Stop wheedling! She is not the type you can —— into making you the beneficiary of her will.

e. What might have been a happy marriage between Romeo and Juliet became instead a tragedy because of a —— between their families.

f. No further misfortunes can befall Stella Dallas, for she is already at the —— of her luck.

g. When Senator Flannellip really gets warmed up to his speech—about ten hours from now—we can be sure that the —— will last for at least a week.

h. His yawl has two masts; our —— has but one.

i. Love is the state in which man sees things most widely different from what they are. The force of illusion reaches its —— here, sweetened and transfigured to new heights.

j. Fame pursues me, but I wish only to be obscure, to be nameless, to move —— among the throng.

vendetta (Italian)	nadir (Arabic)
bas-relief (French)	sloop (Dutch)
incognito (Italian)	peccadillo (Spanish)
zenith (Arabic)	chauvinist (French)
cajole (French)	filibuster (Spanish)

BUILDING VOCABULARY WITH ROOTS

A root (or *stem*) is that part of a word which contains the core of meaning:

fin, meaning "boundary," is the root of such words as:

finish—to bring to an end (or, to bring to the boundary)

finite—measurable (or, having bounds)

infinity—having no bounds

definite—precisely bounded

aster, meaning "star," is the root of such words as:

asterisk—the star-shaped figure used in writing as a mark of reference

astronomy—the law (or, the study of the scientific laws) of the stars

disaster—an unfortunate event (or, something away from the stars. *See note below*)

The greatest number of roots in English derive from the classical languages, Latin and Greek (*fin*, in the example above, is a Latin root; *aster* is a Greek root). By learning several Latin and Greek roots (there are about 160 in all, but you need not try to learn every root), you increase your mastery of words in two important ways:

You will understand more clearly the essential meaning of each part of a word by observing how roots are combined to form words:

nostos, home + *algia*, sickness = *nostalgia*
tele, far off + *phonos*, sound = telephone
epi, upon + *dermis*, skin = epidermis
dia, through + *therme*, heat = diathermy
peri, around + *skopein*, look = periscope
chronos, time + *meter*, measure = chronometer

You will learn words in groups by observing how several words relate to a common root:

equ, equal, just

equal	inequality	equivocable
equate	equity	equinox
equable	adequate	equilibrium
equality	inadequate	equivalent

voc, vok, to call

vocation	avocation	revoke
vociferate	invocation	provoke
vociferous	convoke	evoke
advocate	invoke	

NOTE: Some words, as you have seen, follow the literal meaning of their roots, but others are only secondarily derived. *Astronomy*, for example, means literally *the law of the stars*. But *disaster, away from the stars*, does not literally signify the actual meaning of the word. Thus, you cannot force the literal meaning of the root upon all words. But, as with *disaster*, where the relationship between superstition and misfor-

A SELECTED LIST OF WORDS DERIVED FROM LATIN ROOTS (A)

ROOT	MEANING	CURRENT WORDS
AG agere	do, drive, act	agent, coagulate, actor
AM amo, amare	love	amorous, amatory, amour
ANIM animus	mind, soul, life; intention	animal, animate, unanimous, magnanimous, pusillanimous; animad-version, animosity
BELL bellus	beautiful, fair	belle, belladonna +, belle-lettres
BELL bellum	war	bellicose, belligerent, rebel
CED, CESS cedere, cessus	go, yield	succeed, cede, secede, recede, process, excess, recess, abscess+
CENT centum	hundred	century, centennial
CIT citare	summon arouse	recite, excite, cite, incite
CIV civis	citizen	civic, civilization, civil, civilian
COGNIT cognoscere, cognitus	know	cognizant, incognito, cognition
COR, CORD cor, cordis	heart	core+, accord+, concord+, discord+, cordial, courage
CORP corpus	body	corpse, corps, corporal (punishment), corset, corporation+
CRED credere	believe, credit	credit, creditor, discredit, credible, credence, incredible, incredulous
CULP culpa	offense, fault	culprit, culpable
CUR, CURS cursor, currere	run	current, concourse, cursory+, precursor, discursive+

NOTE: Words whose meanings are secondarily derived from the root are marked +. Use your dictionary to determine the relationship between root and meaning.

tune is implied, you can profit from understanding the correlation between the root meaning and the actual meaning.

You do not need to know Latin or Greek to profit from the tables printed below any more than you need to know Old English, Danish, or French to speak and write effective English.

Learn a few roots at a time and put them to work, first in the exercises, and then in your reading. When you come upon an unfamiliar word like *bicephalous*, don't turn immediately to the dictionary. Ask:

What does it seem to mean in context?

What is the meaning of *bi?* The answer is

A SELECTED LIST OF WORDS DERIVED FROM LATIN ROOTS (B)

ROOT	MEANING	CURRENT WORDS
DEXTER dexter	right hand	dexterous, ambidextrous
DIC, DICT dicere, dictus	say, speak	dictate, predict, contradict, dedicate
DIGN dignus	worthy	dignify, condign, indignity
DUC, DUCE ducere, ductus	lead, bring	ductile, induce, deduce, product, duke, conduit
DUR durus	hard	duress, endure, obdurate+
FAC, FACT facere, factus	do, make, act	fact, factory, facsimile, effect, manufacture, factitious+, factotum
FALL fallere	deceive, err, be deceived	fallacious, fallacy, fallible, infallible
FERR ferre	bear, carry, bring	ferry, infer, transfer, refer, fertile+, suffer, defer
FERV fervere	boil	fervid, effervesce, fervor
GEN, GENER genus, generis	class, kind, race	genus, generic, general, engender, generate
GRAD, GRESS gradi, gressus	walk, go, step	gradual, digress, egress, graduate, transgress, aggression
GRAND grandis	great	aggrandize, grandiose, grandeur
IT ite, itus	go	exit, circuit, itinerant+
JECT jacere, jectus	throw, hurl	deject, inject
JUR jurare	swear	jury, abjure, perjure+
LABOR labor	work	laboratory, elaborate, collaborate, laborious

---

two. What is the meaning of *cephalous?* The answer is *head*.

Thus, you combine reading in context with a knowledge of roots, a significant advance towards word mastery.

NOTE: Almost all the sciences append the root LOGY, the science of:

anthropology	genealogy	pathology
archaeology	geology	philology
bacteriology	histology	physiology
biology	meteorology	psychology
criminology	mythology	theology
demonology	morphology	zoology
entomology	ornithology	

A SELECTED LIST OF WORDS DERIVED FROM LATIN ROOTS (C)

ROOT	MEANING	CURRENT WORDS
LOQU, LOC loquor, locutus	talk, speak	elocution, loquacious, grandiloquent, soliloquy, colloquial, obloquy
MEDI medius	middle, between	immediate+, medieval, mediate, medium
MIT, MISS, MISE mittere, missus	send, throw	emit, permit, commit, omission, permission, dismiss, demise+, missile, missive
MON, MONIT monere, monitus	warn, advise, remind	monument, admonition+, premonition
MOR, MORT mors, mortis	death	mortal, immortal, mortician, mortgage+, mortify
NASC, NAT nascitur	to be born	nascent, natal, nature, renascence
NOMIN nomen	name	name, nomenclature, cognomen, nominate, ignominious, nominal+
NOV novus	new	novel, innovate, novice, novitiate, renovate, novelty
OMNI omnis	all	omniscient, omnipotent, omnipresent, omnibus
PARL parler	speak	parliament, parley, parlance, parlor
PLIC plicare	twine, twist	explicate+, complicate+, implicate+
PONDU pondus	weight	ponderous, imponderable+, preponderance+
PORT portare	carry, bring, bear	portable, transport, porter, export, importance+
RAP, RAPT rapio	seize, grasp	rape, rapine, rapture+, rapacious

A SELECTED LIST OF WORDS DERIVED FROM LATIN ROOTS (D)

ROOT	MEANING	CURRENT WORDS
SED, SESS sedere, sessus	sit	sedentary, reside, sedate, sedan
SPEC, SPECT specere, spectus	look, see, appear	spectacle, prospectus, specie, spectator, conspicuous, introspect, perspicacious
STRING, STRICT stringere, strictus	bind, draw tight	strict, stringent, constrict, restrain, strait, distress
TANG tangere	touch	tangible, contact, tangent
TEN, TIN	hold	tenable, tenure, pertinacity, tenant, tenet
TORT, TORQ torquere	twist	torque, tortuous, distort, retort, torture, contortion
TRACT trahere	draw	abstract+, attract, detract, traction, tractor, protract
VERS, VERT vertere	turn	avert, aversion, adversary, controversy+, extravert, introvert
VIR vir	man	virago, virile, virtuous
VOC, VOK vocare	call	convoke, vocalize, advocate—, vociferous+, avocation—, evoke
VOL velle	wish	volition, benevolence, voluntary, volunteer, malevolent

A SELECTED LIST OF WORDS DERIVED FROM GREEK ROOTS (A)

ROOT	MEANING	CURRENT WORDS
AESTH aisthomal	feel, perceive	aesthetics, esthete, anesthetic+
AGOG agogos	lead, bring	demagogue, synagogue
AGON agon	contest, struggle	protagonist, antagonist, agony
ANTHROP anthropos	man	anthropology, misanthrope, philanthropist, anthropomorphic
ARCH arche	rule, govern	anarchy, archangel, archives, archetype, oligarchy, hierarchy
BIBL biblos, biblion	book	bible, bibliophile, bibliography, bibliomania
BIO bio	life	biology, biography, biotic, biophysics
CHRON chronos	time	chronicle, chronoscope, chronic, chronology, synchronize
DEM demos	people	democrat, demagogue, demotic+, epidemic, endemic
DYNAM dunamos	power	dynamic, aerodynamics, dynamometer, dynamo, dynamite
GAM gamos	marriage	monogamy, polygamy, bigamy, amalgam+
GE geo	earth	geography, geology, geodetic, geometry
GRAPH graphein	write	autograph, biography, graphic+, stenography, phonograph, orthography, graph
HOMO homos	the same	homogenized, homogenous, homonym, homosexual

A SELECTED LIST OF WORDS DERIVED FROM GREEK ROOTS (B)

ROOT	MEANING	CURRENT WORDS
IDIO idios	one's own, peculiar	idiom, idiosyncrasy, idiot+
ISO isos	equal	isosceles, isotope, isobar
KOSM kosmos	universe, order	cosmos, cosmic, cosmography, cosmetic—, cosmopolitan
KRAT kratia	power	democracy, aristocrat, plutocrat, theocrat, bureaucrat
LOG logos	word, speech, science	logic, eulogy, etymology, philology, psychology
METER, METR	measure	diameter, metronome, symmetry
MON, MONO monos	alone	monogamy, monosyllable, monomania, monogram+, monocle+, monolith
NOM nomos	law	deuteronomy, economy
NEO neos	new	neologism, neolithic, neophyte
NEUR neuron	nerve, tendon	neuralgia, neurasthenia, neuritis, neurotic, psychoneurosis
ONYM onyma	name	pseudonym, homonym, anonymous
ORTHO ortho	correct	orthodontia, orthography+, orthodox
PATH pathos	feeling	sympathy, pathos, apathetic, antipathy
PHIL philos	loving, friendly, fond	philanthropist, Philadelphia, philosophy, philharmonic, philology
PHONE phonos	sound	phonetic, telephone, phonology, phonograph, euphony, cacophony
PHYSI physis	nature	physiology+, physicist+, physic, physiognomy

---

Not all words that end in -*logy*, however, refer to sciences: e.g., *analogy, tautology, eulogy, trilogy*. How many others can you name?

BUILDING VOCABULARY WITH PREFIXES AND SUFFIXES

A prefix is a syllable or syllables placed (*fixed*) before (*pre-*) a word to qualify its meaning:

vocation means an occupation or trade, or, literally, *a calling.*

avocation means a hobby, a secondary occupation, or, literally, *away from a calling.*

The meaning of *avocation* has been changed, modified, or qualified by placing before it the prefix *a* (*ab*) meaning *away from.*

A SELECTED LIST OF WORDS DERIVED FROM GREEK ROOTS (C)

ROOT	MEANING	CURRENT WORDS
POLI polis	city	metropolis, politician+, police+, policy+, cosmopolitan+
PSYCHE psyche	mind	psychic, psychology, psychiatry+, psychoanalysis, psychotic+, metempsychosis
PYR pyr	fire	pyre, pyromaniac, pyrotechnics
SCOP skopein	see	scope, telescope, stereoscopic, stethoscope, microscope, bishop+
SOPH sophos	wise	sophomore, philosophy, sophist+, sophisticate+, theosophy
TELE tele	far	telescope, telephone, telegraph, teleology+, telepathy
THERM therme	heat	thermal, thermometer, thermostat
TYP typos	model, impression	typical, archetype, antitype, atypical
TOP topos	a place	topography, topic+, topical+
ZO zoon	animal	zoo, zoology, zodiac+, protozoa

A suffix is a syllable or syllables placed after a word to qualify its meaning:

measure means dimension, size, or quanity.
measurable means capable of being measured.

The meaning of *measurable* has been modified by adding to *measure* the suffix *-able* (*ible*) meaning *capable of being measured.*

Note that the suffix does not change the meaning of a word as drastically as does the prefix, but it does change the grammatical function. Both *avocation* and *vocation* are nouns, but the noun *measure*, because of the addition of the suffix, has become an adjective, *measurable*. Likewise, the adjective *loose* becomes an adverb when the suffix *-ly* is added (*loosely*), and the verb *commit* becomes a noun when the suffix *-sion* is added (*commission*).

NOTE: Certain minor changes in spelling frequently occur. These are intended to make pronunciation easier.

Most of the prefixes and suffixes in modern English derive from Old English, Latin, and Greek. They are so numerous that it is impossible to list all of them, and almost futile to try to learn every one that is listed. However, by learning the strategic affixes, you take another long stride towards improving vocabulary:

By combining your knowledge of roots with knowledge of prefixes and suffixes, you can analyze a surprisingly large number of words:

inscription, for example, breaks down into:
ROOT: *scrip*, meaning write (Latin, *scribere*)
PREFIX: *in*, meaning on (Latin, *in*)
SUFFIX: *-tion*, meaning act of, state of, that which (Latin, *-tion*)

Thus (note that the definition emerges as you work *backward* from SUFFIX to ROOT to PREFIX) *inscription* means literally *the act of writing on.*

A SELECTED LIST OF PREFIXES AND SUFFIXES FROM LATIN (A)

PREFIX	MEANING	CURRENT WORDS
AB- (a-, abs-)	from, away from	abnormal, abduct, absent, avert
AD- (a-, ac-, af-, ag-, al-, an-, ap-, ar-, as-, at-) (these varied forms are used to effect euphonious combinations with the several roots)		
AMBI-	both	ambidextrous, ambivalent, ambiguous
ANTE-	before	antedate, anteroom, antecedent
BI- (bis-)	two, twice	biped, bicycle, bimonthly, bisect
BENE-	good, well	beneficial, benevolent
CIRCUM-	around	circumstance, circumvent, circumnavigate, circumlocution
CON- (com-, co-, col-, cor-)	with	congress, colloquy, coeducation, correlate
CONTRA- (contro-, counter-)	against	contradict, controversy, countermand
DE-	from, down (negative meaning)	denounce, decry, decapitate, debase, degrade
DI- (dis-, dif-)	from, away (negative meaning)	divert, dispel, dismiss, dishonest, differ, diffuse
EQUI-	equal	equanimity, equilateral, equation
EX-	former	ex-president, ex-governor
EX- (e-, ef-, ec-)	out, from, away	exotic, exit, enervate, effulgent, ecstasy
EXTRA-	outside, beyond	extracurricular, extraordinary, extravagant, extraneous
IN- (il-, im-, ir-)	in, into, on (used with verbs and nouns)	intrude, induce, illuminate, import, imbibe, irrigate
IN- (il-, im-, ir-, ig-)	not (used with adjectives)	indecent, illiterate, improper, irreducible, ignoble, ignominious

The context in which the word appears usually makes the meaning more specific:

Walter found the author's *inscription* on the flyleaf.

The tombstone bore the *inscription* of the dead man's date of birth and of death.

By observing the effect **suffixes** have on the words you study, you add depth to your vocabulary by learning several parts of speech derived from a single word:

rational—adjective

rationalism—noun (-*ism* means state of being)

rationalize—verb (-*ize* means to make)

rationally—adverb (-*ly* means similar, or having the quality of)

SOME TECHNIQUES FOR CHANGING PARTS OF SPEECH BY USING PREFIXES AND SUFFIXES

To derive verbs from nouns:

Add the suffix -*ize*

terror—terrorize	drama—dramatize
economy—economize	anesthesia—anesthetize

Add the prefix *en-* or *in-*

slave—enslave	franchise—enfranchise
trench—entrench	grain—ingrain

A SELECTED LIST OF PREFIXES AND SUFFIXES FROM LATIN (B)

PREFIX	MEANING	CURRENT WORDS
INFRA-	under, beneath	infra-red, infra-dig
INTER-	between, among	interurban, international, interchange, interfere, interpose
INTRA-	inside, within	intramural, introvert, introspect, intravenous
MAL- (male-)	bad	malefactor, malevolent, malformed, malocclusion
MULTI-	much, many	multiply, multitude, multicolor
NON-	not (*in-* and *un-* are usually more emphatic)	nonexistent, nonsense, non-Christian
OB- (o-, oc-, of-, op-)	against, out	obstruct, obdurate, obsolete, omit, occult, offend, oppose
PER-	through, throughout	persist, pertinent, perceive, perennial
POST-	after	postpone, postscript, post-graduate
PRE-	before (in *time* or *place*)	precede, predict, prevent, pre-war, prepay
PRO-	forward, in favor of	proceed, provoke, project, propose, pronoun, pro-American
RE-	again, back	repeat, return, remind, recall, refulgent, rebuild, reaffirm
RETRO-	back, backward	retroactive, retrospect, retrogress, retrograde
SINE-	without	sinecure, *sine die*
SUB- (suc-, suf-, sug-, sup-, sus-)	under, beneath	submarine, submerge, succinct, succumb, succubus, suffer, suggest, supplant, suspect
SUPER- (sur-)	above, over	superimpose, superficial, surpass, surfeit
TRANS- (tra-)	across, over	transport, transfer, transmit, traduce, traverse
TRI-	three	triangle, triumvirate
ULTRA-	beyond, outside, unusual, extreme	ultramodern, ultarconservative, ultramarine
UNI-	one	unity, uniform, unilateral, university

To derive nouns from verbs:

Add the suffixes *-tion, -ion, -sion, -ation*

denounce—denunciation compile—compilation
compel—compulsion transpose—transposition

Add the suffixes *-al, -se, -ment, -iture, -ance*

refuse—refusal expend—expense
govern—government buoy—buoyance

Add the suffixes *-er, -or, -ant, -ent*

audit—auditor labor—laborer
expedite—expedient supply—supplicant

To derive adjectives from nouns:

Add the suffixes *-ful, -less, -ious, -ous, -y*

hope—hopeful end—endless beauty—beauteous
sorrow—sorrowful chill—chilly ambition—ambitious

Add the suffixes *-al, -ic, -ish, -an, -ary, -ed*

nature—natural fever—feverish
psychosis—psychotic Sweden—Swedish
imagination—imaginary America—American

To derive nouns from adjectives:

Add the suffixes *-ness, -ity, -ce, -cy*

happy—happiness loquacious—loquacity
romantic—romance fragrant—fragrance

To derive verbs from adjectives:

Add the suffixes *-ize, -en, -fy*

fertile—fertilize   liquid—liquefy
thick—thicken   solid—solidify

To derive adjectives from verbs:

Add the suffixes *-able, -ible, -ive*

reverse—reversible   evade—evasive
manage—manageable   repair—reparable

To derive adverbs from adjectives:

Add the suffix *-ly*

handy—handily   excitable—excitably
angry—angrily   false—falsely

Add the suffix *-wise*

likewise, lengthwise

NOTE: Other suffixes related to parts of speech are listed in the tables below.

By observing the effect *prefixes* have on the words you study, you add depth to your vocabulary by learning *antonyms* (words opposed in meaning, as *good-bad, right-wrong*) for any given word:

rational—irrational (*ir-* means "not," "against")
practical—impractical (*im-* means "not")
ordinary—extraordinary (*extra-* means "in addition to")
territorial—extraterritorial

Learn a few prefixes and suffixes at a time. Put them to work first in the exercises and then in your reading.

Remember:

1. What does the word seem to mean in context?
2. What is the meaning of the root?
3. What is the meaning of the prefix? the suffix?

Combine these bits of knowledge and within a short time, the word will be yours.

NOUN SUFFIXES

GROUP 1: Abstract nouns. These suffixes signify state of, act of, quality of.

SUFFIX	CURRENT WORDS
-ACY	celibacy, democracy
-AGE	bondage, salvage, vassalage, marriage
-ANCE (-ancy, -ence, -ency)	severance, repentance, buoyancy, diligence, emergency
-ATION (-tion, -ion, -sion)	civilization, flirtation, union, dissension
-DOM	freedom, kingdom, serfdom
-HOOD	boyhood, manhood, falsehood
-ICE	avarice, cowardice
-ISM	communism, invalidism, Fascism, baptism
-MENT	government, agreement, statement, payment
-NESS	happiness, lewdness, deafness
-SHIP	partnership, penmanship
-TY (-ity)	security, modesty, femininity

GROUP 2: Concrete nouns. These suffixes signify one who does.

SUFFIX	CURRENT WORDS
-AN (-ant, -ent)	partisan, artisan, participant, equestrian, vagrant, student
-ARD (-art, -ary)	drunkard, braggart, notary
-EE (-eer, -ess)	legatee, auctioneer, tigress
-ER (-ar, -ier, -or)	laborer, scholar, clothier, auditor
-IC (-ist, -ite, -yte)	nomadic, sadist, Brooklynite, acolyte

ADJECTIVE SUFFIXES

GROUP 1. These suffixes signify resembling, full of, or belonging to.

Suffix	Current Words
-AC (-al, -an, -ar, -ary)	cardiac, seasonal, vernal, Russian, circular, imaginary
-FUL	spiteful, vengeful, hateful
-IC (-ical)	anemic, inimical, maniacal
-ISH	foolish, English, childish
-IVE	restive, furtive, secretive
-ORY	admonitory, hortatory
-OUS	mendacious, gracious, efficacious
-ULENT	succulent, fraudulent

A SELECTED LIST OF PREFIXES AND SUFFIXES FROM GREEK

PREFIXES

Prefix	Meaning	Current Words
A- (an-)	not, without	apathetic, aseptic, atheism, anarchy
AMPHI-	about, around, on both sides	amphitheater, amphibious
ANA-	again, up, against	anachronism, analogy, analogue
ANTI- (ant-)	opposed, against	antonym, anticlimax, antidote, anti-war
ARCH- (archi-)	chief, primitive (the earliest)	architect, archbishop, archangel
AUTO-	self	autocrat, automobile, autochthonous
CATA-	down, downward	catalepsy, cataclysm, catastrophe
DIA-	through, between	diathermy, dialogue, diagram, diameter, diagonal
EC-	from, out of	eccentric, ecstatic
EPI- (ep-, eph-)	upon, beside	epidemic, epilogue, ephemeral, epileptic
EU-	good, happy, well	euphony, eugenic, euthanasia, eulogy
HETERO-	different	heterogeneous, heterodox
HOMO-	the same	homogenous, homonym, homosexual
HYPER-	extreme, over, above	hypersensitive, hyperbole
HYPO-	under, below	hypocrite, hypodermic, hypochondriac, hypothesis
META-	after, beyond	metathesis, metaphysics, metabolism
NEO-	new	neologism, neophyte, neoclassical
PARA-	beside	paraphrase, paradox, parallel
PERI-	around, about	perimeter, periscope, peripatetic
POLY-	many	polygamy, polygon, polysyllable
PRO-	to, towards, before	prologue, program, proselyte
SYN- (sym-, syl-)	with, together	synagogue, synonym, synopsis, symmetry, sympathy, symphony, syllogism, syllable

SUFFIXES

Suffix	Meaning	Current Words
-ISE (-ize)	to make, give	synthesize, tantalize, criticize
-OID	like	spheroid, negroid, anthropoid

GROUP 2. These suffixes signify **capable, able to.**

-ABLE	movable, curable, peaceable
-IBLE	irresistible, visible
-ILE	ductile, puerile, fertile

VERB SUFFIXES

These suffixes signify **to make.**

-ATE	procreate, animate, perpetuate, facilitate
-EN	moisten, deepen, loosen, quicken
-FY	qualify, fortify, stupefy
-IZE (-ise)	magnetize, criticise, sterilize, fertilize

Review Work on Roots, Prefixes, and Suffixes

For each of the following words, add appropriate prefixes and suffixes to create as many derivative words as possible. Keep the same stem throughout. Be certain of the meaning of each derivative word.

EXAMPLE: *compel* (Lat. pellere, pulsus, to drive)

Derivative words from *compel*

Nouns	Verbs	Adjectives	Adverbs
compulsion	compel	compulsory	compulsorily
		compulsive	

A SELECTED LIST OF PREFIXES AND SUFFIXES FROM ANGLO-SAXON

PREFIXES

Prefix	Meaning	Current Words
A-	at, in, on, to	ahead, asleep, afoot, aground
BE-	throughout, over	bedaub, bedeck, besmudge, besiege
BE-	by, in	because, beside
FOR-	against, not	forbid, forbear, forlorn
FORE-	before	foretell, foreground, forehead
MIS-	error, defect, wrong	mistake, mislay, misbehavior, misconduct
OUT-	beyond, completely	outdo, outside, outbreak
UN-	not	untie, undo, uninspired
UNDER-	beneath, less than	underwrite, undertow, underrate
UP-	high	upshot, uplift, upset
WITH-	from, against	withstand, withdraw, withhold

SUFFIXES

Suffix	Meaning	Current Words
-DOM	condition	freedom, wisdom
-FOLD	number, quantity	tenfold, manifold
-LESS	lacking, wanting	helpless, thoughtless
-LING	related to, belonging to	yearling, gosling, foundling
-LY	like, similar	hopefully, meagerly, evenly, closely
-MOST	(indicates superlative degree)	foremost, hindmost, inmost
-TH	state of, quality of	wealth, dearth, warmth
-WARD	in the direction of	northward, inward, outward
-WISE	way, manner	lengthwise, crosswise, otherwise
-Y	similar, pertaining to	greedy, nosy, bony, slimy

repulsion	repel	repellent	repulsively
	dispell		
pulsation	pulsate	pulsatory	
pulse			
pulsometer			
propellor	propel		
propulsion			
impulse	impel	impulsive	impulsively

describe (*scribere*, write)
factor (*facere*, make, do)
pathos (*pathos*, feeling)
dependent (*pendere, -pensus*, to hang)
graphic (*graphos*, write)
spirit (*spirare*, to breathe)
sage (*sagire*, to discern)
vitalize (*vita*, life)
philology (*philos*, love)
chronicle (*chronos*, time)

LEARNING THE ORIGIN OF WORDS

Knowing the root of a word sometimes fails to produce a logical meaning. The root of *salary*, for example, is *sal*, meaning "salt," a far cry from our usage today. Yet if one thinks for a moment of a common expression such as "He is not worth his salt," he must realize that somewhere in the history of that root, a connection existed between money and salt. The connection dates back to the days of the Roman Empire when Roman soldiers were often paid for their services with enough money to buy the salt they needed for personal use. Thus what they earned was literally "salt money."

The search for the historical origins of words is called etymology (*etymos*, the real, or true + *logos*, the study of). The realms of etymology may be fully explored only by the professional philologist (See Skeat's *Etymological Dictionary of the English Language*), but the amateur can have considerable and profitable fun tracing words as far back as he can.

Other examples:

CARTRIDGE—French, *cartouche*, Latin, *carta*. The Latin word, *carta*, means "paper," and the later French *cartouche* likewise meant a paper scroll on which messages were written. The first cartridges used in guns were rolled cylinders made of heavy paper; their resemblance to the letter scroll earned them the name *cartouche*, whence modern English *cartridge*.

DANDELION—French, *dent de lion* (teeth of a lion). The petals of the flower resemble teeth.

JIN-RIKISHA—Japanese. Here the roots provide the literal meaning of the word:

> *jin* = man
> *riki* = power
> *sha* = carriage

EXCHEQUER—French, *eschequier*, chessboard. Edward I, King of England in the thirteenth century, handled all of his financial matters across a checkered table. The custom continued in England through the nineteenth century.

CHAPLAIN—French, *capa*; Latin, *capa*. Whenever the ancient kings of France went to war, they carried with them the cape of St. Martin of Tours. Wherever they set up camp, they kept his cape in a tent (*capella*) where it was guarded by a *chapelain*.

See what your dictionary tells about these words:

pastor	strafe	tawdry
congregation	daisy	grammar
eliminate	silly	hysteria
curfew	alphabet	taboo
assassin	hors d'oeuvre	nosegay
neighbor	phlegmatic	trivial

WORDS DERIVED FROM PROPER NAMES

Do you know these people?

Jean Nicot	J. A. Hansom
John Mercer	Vulcan
Amelia Bloomer	James Watt
Pierre Magnol	Thespis
Tantalus	Hector

Each of them has given a word to the English language.

Jean Nicot—introduced tobacco to France in 1560—*nicotine*.

John Mercer—discovered a way to make cotton stronger for use as thread—*mercerize*.

Amelia Bloomer—designed a gown to fit over ankle-length pantaloons—*bloomers*.

Pierre Magnol—French botanist—*magnolia*.

Tantalus—the king in Greek mythology condemned to reach for fruit ever beyond his grasp, and for water which receded when he sought to slake his thirst—*tantalize*.

J. A. Hansom—inventor of the *hansom cab*.

Vulcan—the Roman god of fire—*vulcanize*.

James Watt—scientist who worked in electrical measurements—*watt*.

Thespis—Greek poet responsible for the drama—*thespian*.

Hector—Trojan warrior, brave, but a bully—*hector* (to torment or bully).

Look up the following words:

roentgenology	quixotic	rodomontade
ampere	stentorian	simony
volt	dunce	Rosicrucian
wisteria	daguerreotype	maudlin
maverick	herculean	

PORTMANTEAU WORDS, OR BLENDED WORDS

Words, like the contents of a valise (*portmanteau*) sometimes get squeezed together to form a new word:

> lunch + breakfast = brunch
> chuckle + snort = chortle
> dance + handle = dandle

Lewis Carroll's "Jabberwocky" in *Alice Through the Looking Glass* is the finest example of the imaginative use of **blended words**:

> slithy from *slimy* and *lithe*
> mimsy from *flimsy* and *miserable*
> nome from *far from* and *home*

SUMMARY OF METHODS OF BUILDING VOCABULARY

1. Learn only those words that you intend to use.
2. Keep a notebook or file card collection of new words.
3. Use the dictionary.
4. Try to recognize the use of the word in context.
5. Learn roots, prefixes, and suffixes.
6. Convert each new word into other parts of speech.
7. Be curious about word origins and changes in word meaning.
8. Study your words daily and *use* them in writing and speaking.

Paperbound Dictionaries

American Heritage Dictionary of the English Language (Dell).

Funk and Wagnall's Standard Dictionary (NAL/Signet).

The Merriam-Webster Dictionary (Pocket Books, Inc.).

The Oxford English Dictionary (Avon).

The Random House Dictionary (Ballantine).

The Scribner-Bantam English Dictionary (Bantam).

Webster's New World Dictionary of the American Language (Popular Library).

Webster's New World Dictionary of the American Language (New American Library).

ANSWERS

ANSWERS

Exercise No. 1

1. literature
2. Arctic
3. recognize
4. chocolate
5. athlete
6. irrelevant
7. interesting
8. every
9. marriage
10. temperature

Exercise No. 2

1. c   3. b   5. b   7. c   9. c
2. a   4. a   6. c   8. c   10. a

Exercise No. 3

1. a   3. c   5. b   7. c   9. b
2. c   4. a   6. c   8. a   10. o

Exercise No. 4

1. e   4. i   7. e   10. i   13. i
2. i   5. o   8. e   11. i   14. e
3. y   6. o   9. i   12. e   15. a

Exercise No. 5

buoy-ant, chang-ing, coun-try, criti-cism, run-ning, pas-sage, dwin-dling, siz-zling, exces-sive. None of the other words should be divided.

Exercise No. 6

a. anti-vivisectionism
   single-minded
b. mop-up
   pro-United States
   middle road
c. night-time
d. all-night
   knee-deep
   two-thirds
e. All-cargo
   on-time
   eighty-three
   trans-shipment

Note: *heavily traveled* is not hyphenated because *heavily* modifies traveled; it does not combine with it to modify *section*.

Exercise No. 7

a. trays   e. swans   i. kisses   m. albatrosses
b. pies   f. waxes   j. snappers   n. mosses
c. ashes   g. gnus   k. grasses   o. taxes
d. lynxes   h. ostriches   l. eels

ashen, waxen, kissable, mossy, taxable, grassy

Exercise No. 8

a. silos
b. shelves
c. knives
d. calves
e. sheriffs
f. rabbis
g. hoofs
h. muffs
i. embargoes
j. gulfs

Exercise No. 9

a. radius
b. cherub
c. virtuoso
d. phenomenon
e. medium
f. vertebra
g. dilettante
h. chateau
i. stigma
j. focus

Exercise No. 10

a. flashes
b. Negroes
c. scissors
d. agenda
e. datum
f. teaspoonfuls
g. passers-by
h. calves
i. embargoes
j. dynamos
k. themselves
l. roofs
m. gnus
n. matches
o. foxes
p. oxen
q. loaves
r. wives
s. crises
t. innuendoes

Exercise No. 11

a. drunk
b. burst
c. sworn
d. lay
e. begun
f. stung
g. slew, slain
h. did, have done
i. awoke, forsaken
j. bidden

147

Exercise No. 12

a. attacks. Subject is *One.*
b. confuses. Subject is *Learning.*
c. add. Subject is *Candlelight and wine.*
d. were. Subject is *Bill and Ed.*
e. has. Subject is *set.*
f. suffers. Subject is *each.*
g. need. Subject is *who* which refers to the plural *girls.*
h. likes. Subject is *Neither,* which is singular.
i. understands. Same as h.
j. knows. Subject is *Everybody.*

Exercise No. 13

1. dissonance
2. misshapen
3. mishap
4. correct
5. dissuade
6. disappointed
7. correct
8. misstatement
9. commissioner
10. competent, dissimilar

Exercise No. 14

1. digress
2. irrigate
3. succumbed
4. ignoble
5. imbibes
6. supplant
7. allocated
8. adjudicated
9. submarine, submerged
10. difference

Exercise No. 15

1. antecedents
2. persist
3. divulge
4. antiseptic
5. precedes
6. professor
7. antidote
8. disease
9. description
10. despair

Exercise No. 16

1. adolescence
2. subsistence
3. interference
4. ignorant
5. extravagant
6. resonant
7. inference
8. tolerant
9. hesitant
10. reference

Exercise No. 17

1. curable
2. intangible
3. invincible
4. deplorable
5. blamable
6. plausible
7. irascible
8. amicable
9. reducible
10. demonstrable
11. visible
12. predictable
13. inaudible
14. acceptable
15. immovable

Exercise No. 18

1. chastised
2. debtors
3. liquefy
4. devise
5. consumer
6. beautify
7. criticize
8. employer
9. really
10. recognize
11. Senator
12. basically
13. accidentally
14. truthfully
15. testify

Exercise No. 19

1. *mis,* "send, throw." One who is *sent* on a specific mission.
2. *ten,* "hold." A firm, tough *hold.*
3. *ten,* "hold." A point of view that cannot be logically *held.* Un- means "not."
4. *mis,* "send," and *de-,* "away." A sending away, or, as here, an unfortunate ending, or death.
5. *mis,* "send," and *sur-,* "above, upon." A "sending upon," or, as here, a guess based *upon* evidence *sent* from various inconclusive sources.
6. *mis,* "send." An object *thrown* or sent in a directed path.
7. *log,* "speech," and *eu-,* "happy." A *speech* delivered to praise a person, event, or thing.
8. *auto,* "self," and *nomos,* "law." A state which is *self-*governed.
9. *tin,* "hold," *in-,* "not," *con-,* "together." Literally, "one who cannot hold himself together"; here, one who cannot control his drinking.
10. *auto,* "self," *kratos,* "rule, power." A *self-*determined despot who is a *law* only unto *himself.*

Exercise No. 20

1. synonyms
2. aggrandize
3. expatriates
4. adjudicate
5. efficacious

Exercise No. 21

a. disenchant
b. dishonorable
c. unethical
d. illiterate
e. infallible
f. irrational
g. disagree
h. misconduct
i. disquiet
j. disengage

Exercise No. 22

a. hypnotism, hypnotic
b. comprehension, comprehensible
c. equivocation, equivocable
d. liquefaction
e. criticism, critical
f. navigation, navigable

g. certification, certifiable
h. analysis, analyzable
i. mechanization
j. effervescence, effervescent

Exercise No. 23

a. apprehend, apprehensive   f. admire, admirable
b. liberate, liberal   g. ignite, igneous
c. consummate (verb and adj.) h. malicious
d. diffident   i. gratuitous
e. medicate, medicant   j. regulate, regulative

Exercise No. 24

a. categorize, category   d. paternalize, paternalism
b. hypothecate, hypothesis   e. facetiously
c. materialize, materialism

Exercise No. 25

1. gentlemen's
2. o'
3. hero's
4. they're
5. sun's
6. you'll
7. Melissa's
8. Twain's
9. boys' clothes
10. Achilles'
11. Wales'
12. Who's
13. yeomen's
14. nobody's
15. nobody's
16. Libby's
17. princesses'
18. *William's* if the given name is intended;
    Williams' if the surname is intended.
19. here's
20. children's

Exercise No. 26

The passage should read: *She's* the kind of woman who thinks that *everybody's* problems are *hers*. Well, we *don't* need her help. Other *people's* notions apply to *their* special needs: *everybody's* situation has *its* special quirk. *It's* time we regarded our problem as *ours*, not *anybody else's*. *Whose* solution *would've* been better *we'll* not know for many years, but at least *ours* will be *yours* and mine, not *hers*.

Exercise No. 27

1. The Anglo-Saxon language was the language of our Saxon forefathers in England, though they never gave it that name. They called it English. Thus King Alfred speaks of translating "from book-Latin into English"; Abbot Aelfric was requested by Aethelward "to translate the book of Genesis from Latin into English"; and Bishop Leofric, speaking of the manuscript (the "Exeter Manuscript") he gave to Exeter Cathedral, calls it a "great English book."

2. The city of Nome, Alaska, acquired its name through error. There was a small prospectors' settlement known as Anvil City on the Seward Peninsula in Alaska. A Washington clerk, in drawing a map, did not know its name, and wrote "Name?" at that place on the map. One of his superiors took the word for "Nome" and that name still stands.

3. *Stories in the Modern Manner*, edited by Philip Rahv and William Phillips, was published by Avon Books. Perhaps the best story in it is Gide's "Theseus."

4. The lion is a kingly beast.
   He likes a Hindu for a feast.

5. It is the grace of God that urges missionaries to suffer the most disheartening privations for their faith. This grace moved Saint Isaac Jogues to say (when he came to Canada), "I feel as if it were a Christmas day for me, and that I was to be born again to a new life, to a life in Him." (Adapted from *Time*)

Exercise No. 28

1. heinous	5. fiend	9. sleigh	13. fierce
2. cashier	6. bier	10. feign	14. yield
3. inveigh	7. wield	11. skein	15. achieve
4. deign	8. tier	12. reprieve	

Exercise No. 29

1. grief	6. quotient
2. deity	7. glacier
3. heifer	8. conscience
4. species	9. gaiety
5. weird	10. either, neither

11. transient
12. foreign
13. inveigled
14. receipt
15. vein
16. wield
17. shriek
18. veiled
19. seizure
20. neighbor
21. reins
22. sheik
23. patient
24. sobriety
25. relief
26. priestly, hierarchy
27. proficient
28. eider
29. deficiency
30. counterfeit
31. sovereign
32. leisure
33. deceitful
34. alien
35. medieval
36. surfeited
37. ancient
38. quiet
39. mischief
40. chief
41. perceive
42. brief
43. ceiling
44. field
45. pier
46. fiery
47. friend
48. omniscient
49. mien
50. financier

Exercise No. 30

1. usable
2. dining
3. movable
4. having
5. conceivable
6. likelihood
7. admirable
8. surely
9. likeable
10. careless
11. salable
12. coming
13. loneliness
14. mistakable
15. desirable

Exercise No. 31

1. dyeing
2. judging
3. toeing
4. duly, argued
5. lovely
6. singeing
7. singing
8. advantageous
9. agreeing
10. pursuing
11. courageous
12. desirable
13. changeable
14. truly
15. shoeing
16. dying
17. outrageous
18. serviceable
19. swingeing
20. usage

Exercise No. 32

1. trolleys
2. families
3. employs
4. valleys
5. copies
6. slain
7. plied
8. cries
9. played
10. marrying
11. hurrying
12. satisfied
13. turkeys
14. married
15. daily
16. relies
17. journeys
18. enjoys
19. keys
20. buries

Exercise No. 33

1. winning
2. studying
3. boiling
4. dryness
5. quitting
6. forbidding
7. coming
8. marvelous
9. traveled
10. mysterious
11. business
12. changeable
13. tries
14. babies
15. daily
16. whipping
17. committed
18. preference
19. runner
20. stabbed
21. filling
22. unmistakably
23. bragging
24. skies
25. cries
26. noticeable
27. ceiling
28. stopping
29. occurrence
30. reference
31. writing
32. gripping
33. inconquerable
34. coyness
35. marriage
36. envious
37. plies
38. keys
39. armies
40. laid
41. lay
42. laid
43. lain
44. counseled
45. denied
46. sitting
47. omitted
48. beginner's
49. ladies
50. mannish

Exercise No. 34

1. b	5. a	9. c	13. c	17. a
2. a	6. c	10. a	14. a	18. b
3. c	7. a	11. b	15. b	19. a
4. c	8. b	12. a	16. c	20. b

Exercise No. 35

The number in parentheses refers to the chapter in which appears the rule applicable to the spelling.

1. Hilda's (8)
2. Judaism (8)
3. dining (10)
4. correct (8)
5. Joneses' (8)
6. you'll (8)
7. should've (8)
8. Negro's (8)
9. dyed (10)
10. concedes (11)
11. Nome, Alaska (8)
12. Max's (8)
13. picnicking (11)
14. vein (9)
15. laid (10)
16. exceed (11)
17. civilian (11)
18. villain (11)
19. mountain (11)
20. conceived (9)
21. y's (8)
22. panicked (11)
23. correct (8)
24. History (8)
25. ceiling (9)
26. proficient (9)
27. Father (8)
28. English (8)
29. truly (10)
30. razor's (8)
31. they'd (8)
32. correct (10)
33. Monday's (8)
34. patient (9)
35. outrageous (10)
36. leisure (9)
37. Dickens' (8)
38. financier (9)
39. it's (8)
40. correct (8)

41. correct (8)
42. guardian's (8, 11)
43. correct (8)
44. o'clock (8)
45. yield (9)

46. you're (8)
47. martial (11)
48. Here's (8)
49. auxiliary (11)
50. Christian (8, 11)

3. site
4. deprecate, dessert
5. council, counseled, device
6. idle, forth
7. croquet, crotchets
8. fowl, climactic
9. immigrants', descent
10. dining, elicit

Exercise No. 36

1. berth
2. bridal
3. excess
4. assent
5. Briton, accept

6. capitol, capital
7. alter
8. illusions
9. averse, advice
10. effect, altogether, affected, beside

Exercise No. 38

1. reign, morals
2. led, too, quiet
3. principal, peace
4. personal, past
5. respectfully, right, stationery

6. plain, led
7. who's
8. you're, weak, then
9. threw, straight
10. lose, veins

Exercise No. 37

1. coarse
2. eminent, ingenuous

MASTERY TEST ANSWERS

Mastery Test No. 1

I.

1. b. Note that *its'* does not exist in our language. *It's* means *it is.*
2. a. *Too* means *also.*
3. b. *They're* means *they are. Their* is a possessive pronoun, as in *their books. There* is an adverb denoting "place."
4. a.
5. a.
6. c.
7. b.
8. a.
9. a.
10. a.

II.

1. occurred   3. accommodate   5. Definitely
2. business   4. occasion

III.

1. definition   2. existence   3. to   4. to   5. Forty

IV.

1. occur   4. believe   7. achievement
2. losing   5. busy   8. separate
3. receive   6. all right   9. criticism
              10. realize

V.

belief, achieve, definite.

The correct and incorrect forms of *receiving, occurring,* and *occurrence* have been reversed. The same is true of *exist.* Only with *existence* is the incorrect spelling placed as it should be. Thus, this group of words should read as follows:

recieving for *receiving; occuring* and *occurence* for *occurring* and *occurrence;* and *exsist* and *existance* for *exist* and *existence.*

Mastery Test No. 2

I.

1. written	4. interest	7. environment
2. athletic	5. shining	8. similar
3. surprise	6. government	9. among
		10. beginning

II.

1. whether, weather   3. affect, effect
2. chose, choose, effective 4. personal, personnel
                             5. women

III.

1. governor, writing   4. thorough
2. interpretation, condemn   5. benefit
3. marriage, beneficial, disastrous

IV.

athlete, interpret, choice, than, benefited, write

Mastery Test No. 3

I.

1. exaggerate	4. noticeable	7. acquaint
2. Immediately	5. privilege	8. conscious
3. incidentally	6. possession	9. loneliness
		10. necessary

II.

1. prejudice	4. conscientious	7. performance
2. intelligent	5. controversial	8. description
3. experience	6. acquaintance	9. comparative
		10. perform

III.

1. describe, profession   4. category, succeed
2. probably, controversy   5. using, psychology
3. incident, repetition

IV.

lonely, professor, success, explanation, useless, immediate, useful, recommend, possess

IV.

independent, prefers, refer, predominant, conceive, arising, proceeding

Mastery Test No. 4

I.

1. embarrass
2. prominent
3. imagine
4. foreign
5. appearance

II.

1. led, lead
2. passed, past
3. advice, advise
4. sense, principle, principal
5. varies, various

III.

1. apparent
2. approach
3. heroes
4. imaginary
5. foreigners
6. pursue
7. prevalent
8. analyze
9. consistent
10. rhythm

IV.

A. hero, Negroes, imagination, consistency, heroic, Negro
B. heroine, height, grammar, tried, approaches, tries, studying, analysis

Mastery Test No. 5

I.

1. opponent
2. opinion
3. exercise
4. characterize
5. disappoint
6. preferred
7. procedure
8. difference
9. irresistible
10. irrelevant

II.

1. referred
2. conceivable
3. characteristic
4. convenience
5. efficiency
6. optimism
7. irritable
8. maintenance
9. considerably
10. guidance

III.

1-i (oppose) 4-e (efficiency) 7-a
2-g (arise) 5-f 8-b (independence)
3-d (different) 6-j (opportunity) 9-c (precede)
10-h (character)

Mastery Test No. 6

I.

1-f (psychopathic)   6-h (subtle)
2-g (psychoanalysis) 7-c (temperament)
3-a   8-d (villain)
4-i (tragedy)   9-j (summary)
5-b (hypocrite)   10-e (sophomore)

II.

1. argument
2. original
3. humorous
4. hypocrisy
5. philosophy
6. hindrance
7. ridicule
8. satire
9. summed
10. suppress

III.

1. controlled
2. tyranny
3. aggressive
4. suppose
5. unusual
6. techniques
7. therefore
8. unusually
9. humorist
10. sergeants

IV.

Further, arguing, propagates, propaganda, ridiculous, propaganda, fulfil (or fulfill), together, origin, satirize

Mastery Test No. 7

I.

1. academically
2. accessible
3. acceptance
4. acceptable
5. accidental
6. accidentally
7. basically
8. finally
9. fundamental
10. fundamentally

II.

1. decision
2. Academy
3. access
4. Christianity
5. Britannica
6. accident
7. across
8. challenge
9. curiosity
10. discipline

III.

1. Britain
2. academic
3. Christian
4. Lengthening
5. basis
6. coming
7. Familiar
8. curious
9. disciples
10. accept

IV.

decided, article, doesn't, strength, accepting, length, strengthen, you're, speaking, Christ, etc.

Mastery Test No. 8

I.

1. friend
2. weird
3. atheist
4. chief
5. deceiver
6. field
7. financiers
8. gaiety
9. leisure
10. perceive
11. seize
12. view
13. yield
14. piece
15. relieve

II.

1. Financially
2. leisurely
3. attendant
4. authoritative
5. before
6. Careless
7. knowledge
8. laboratory
9. livelihood
10. ninety
11. authority
12. careful
13. happiness
14. influential
15. Liveliness

III.

author's friendliness, attendance, lives, attended, liveliest, influence, dependent

Mastery Test No. 9

I.

1. carrying
2. carrier
3. desirability
4. extremely
5. accompanied
6. advantageous
7. applies
8. changeable
9. companies
10. countries

II.

1. omitted
2. swimming
3. buried
4. transferred
5. parallel
6. connotes
7. accompanying
8. carried
9. counselor
10. sufficient

III.

1. particular
2. theories
3. stories
4. sincerely
5. connotation
6. changing
7. applying
8. accompaniment
9. desire
10. company

IV.

bury, omit, story, accompanies, carries, theory, advantage, council, consel, permit

Mastery Test No. 10

I.

1-e (alleviate)
2-g (stabilization)
3-a (concede)
4-j (allotment)
5-c (accurate)
6-f (amateur)
7-b (sponsor)
8-h (susceptible)
9-d (aggravate)
10-i (significance)

II.

1. continuous
2. paid
3. physical
4. undoubtedly
5. Accuracy
6. admittance
7. allotted
8. Tomorrow
9. tremendous
10. warrant

III.

1. planned
2. pleasant
3. possible
4. quantity
5. accomplish
6. admission
7. afraid
8. allowed
9. religion
10. response

IV.

altar, Those, thought, speech, vengeance, against, accurately, admit, allows

Mastery Test No. 11

I.

1. already, quiet
2. Altogether, all together
3. cite, device
4. due, except
5. hear, here
6. ingenious, later
7. loss, loose
8. moral, morale
9. prophesy, peace, prophecy
10. whole, scene

II.

1-j

2-e

3-a (symbol)

4-b (accuser)

5-h (calendar)

6-d (annual)

7-c (adolescent)

8-i (dilemma)

9-g (permanent)

10-f (apology)

III.

1. mora*lly*
2. ac*cuses*
3. Adole*s*cence
4. Annua*lly*
5. bri*lli*ant
6. cigare*tte*
7. cor*re*late
8. di*ffi*cult
9. o*ff*
10. who*se*

IV.

phase (fase), accusing, apologized, where, source, And, brilliance, mere, amount, dining

Mastery Test No. 12

I.

1-c (abundance)

2-e (acclaim)

6-h (competition)

7-j (genius)

3-f

4-i (cemetery)

5-d (advertising)

8-g (huge)

9-b (hundred)

10-a (apparatus)

II.

1. Absence
2. adund*a*nt
3. ad*e*quately
4. advertis*er*
5. appre*c*iate
6. competi*t*or
7. d*i*vide
8. e*s*cape
9. idea
10. me*di*cine

III.

1. accustom
2. actually
3. advertisement
4. children
5. hoping
6. dissatisfied
7. especially
8. literature
9. presence
10. eighth

IV.

A. entertainment, During, themselves, another, easily, every, actual, practice, Maybe, divine

B. politician, area, plausible, sentence, safety, laid, actuality, dealt, hopeless

SPECIAL WORD ANSWERS

Special Word Exercise No. 1
I.
1. tariff
2. merchandise, ledger
3. management, franchise

II.
1. auditor, embezzled
2. collateral
3. negotiable
4. personnel

III.
1. promissory, dunning
2. accountant
3. coupons

IV.
1. syndicate
2. entrepreneur
3. mortgage, acknowledgment
4. liquidate

Special Word Exercise No. 2
I.
1. bigamy, annul
2. abandonment, alimony
3. accessory

II.
1. defendant, alibi
2. indictment, burglary
3. coercion

III.
1. bankrupt, affidavit
2. writ, counsellor-at-law
3. subpoena

IV.
1. adjudicate
2. bailiff, arraign, homicide
3. usury

Special Word Exercise No. 3
I.
1. amphibians
2. zoology, embryo, botany, fungus

II.
1. carnivorous
2. vertebrate, mammal
3. evolution, parasite

III.
1. microscope, organism
2. anatomy, heredity
3. instinct

IV.
1. Chlorophyll
2. bacilli
3. protoplasm, carbohydrate
4. chromosome

Special Word Exercise No. 4
I.
1. catarrh
2. adenoids, laryngitis
3. allery, antiseptic

II.
1. virus, vaccine
2. antibiotics
3. diagnosis, obstetrics

III.
1. pediatrician
2. hormone, eczema
3. antitoxin, hemorrhage

IV.
1. astigmatism
2. cardiology
3. inoculate, paralysis
4. epilepsy

Special Word Exercise No. 5

I.

1. nuclear fission
2. cyclotron
3. amplifier, fidelity
4. cathode ray

II.

1. Cosmic rays
2. supersonic
3. abacus, infinity
4. electronics

III.

1. integer, decimal
2. numerator, denominator
3. quotient

IV.

1. circumference, angle, isosceles
2. hypotenuse
3. perpendicular

Special Word Exercise No. 6

I.

1. ballet, choreography
2. arabesque, pirouette, entrechat

II.

1. abstraction
2. surrealism
3. gouache
4. chiaroscuro
5. ceramic

III.

1. fugue, counterpoint
2. madrigal
3. symphony
4. rhapsody

IV.

1. atonality, dissonance
2. a capella
3. cadence, staccato

Special Word Exercise No. 7

I.

1. autobiography
2. novel, essay
3. comedy, tragedy

II.

1. Realism, romanticism
2. Naturalism
3. classicism
4. satire

III.

1. bibliography, drama
2. picaresque, narrative
3. soliloquy

IV.

1. lyric
2. imagery
3. prologue, rhythm, rhyme

Special Word Exercise No. 8

I.

1. anxiety
2. psychoanalysis, psychiatry
3. Oedipus complex, transference

II.

1. repression, hysteria
2. claustrophobia, amnesia
3. senility

III.

1. psychosomatic
2. Paranoid
3. inhibitions
4. neurosis, psychosis

IV.

1. empirical
2. aptitude, intelligence
3. sublimation
4. rapport

Special Word Exercise No. 9

I.

1. façade, baroque
2. Gothic
3. Romanesque
4. gargoyles

II.

1. abutments
2. girder
3. lancet, nave
4. rotunda

III.

1. Byzantine
2. colonnades
3. buttresses
4. corridor, mosaic

IV.

1. wainscot, veneer
2. trellis
3. cornice
4. cantilever

Special Word Exercise No. 10

I.

1. Judaism, Christianity, Bible
2. Buddhism, Mohammedanism

II.

1. orthodox, sacrilegious, atheism, blasphemy, deity

III.

1. gospel
2. catechism
3. baptism
4. theology, parochial

IV.

1. Crucifixion
2. prophets, congregation, parable
3. disciple

Special Word Exercise No. 11

I.

1. hypertension, barbiturate
2. streptomycin, penicillin, antihistamine

II.

1. jet propulsion, aggression
2. fissionable
3. racism, genocide

III.

1. telecast, documentary, nylon
2. Frequency modulation
3. collage

IV.

1. technological, prefabricated, streamlined
2. Existentalism
3. extrasensory

ANSWERS TO FINAL TEST

1. losing
2. proceed
3. height
4. opinion
5. writing
6. professor
7. therefore
8. foreign
9. marriage
10. all right
11. heroes
12. referred
13. amateur
14. atheist
15. ninety
16. advertisement
17. leisure
18. laboratory
19. irresistible
20. description
21. efficient
22. rhythm
23. embarrass
24. environment
25. exaggerate
26. prevalent
27. irrelevant
28. occurrence
29. accidentally
30. adolescence
31. weird
32. advantageous
33. parallel
34. immediately
35. beneficial
36. criticism
37. occasion
38. loneliness
39. characteristic
40. belief
41. accommodate
42. disappoint
43. grammar
44. athlete
45. interest
46. controversial
47. separate
48. maintenance
49. argument
50. villain

37. occasion
38. rhythm
39. athletic
40. independence
41. comparative
42. beneficial
43. opportunity
44. interest
45. exaggerate
46. hypocrisy
47. different
48. irritable
49. temperament
50. effective

Part II:

1. strength
2. amicable
3. antecedent
4. Arctic
5. background
6. buoyant
7. temperature
8. calves
9. chastise
10. chateau
11. chocolate
12. college
13. commissioner
14. competent
15. consummate
16. crisis
17. curable
18. demonstrable
19. deplorable
20. despair
21. divulge
22. diary
23. diffident
24. digress
25. dilettante
26. dynamo
27. efficacious
28. embargo
29. exactly
30. frivolous
31. gratuitous
32. hesitant
33. ignorant
34. illiterate
35. immovable
36. innuendo
37. invincible
38. knives
39. liquefy
40. mathematics
41. miniature
42. mysterious
43. parliament
44. plausible
45. recognize
46. reducible
47. reference
48. scissors
49. shelves
50. succumb

ANSWERS TO HALFWAY TEST

Part I:

1. losing
2. proceed
3. opinion
4. writing
5. professor
6. existence
7. foreign
8. business
9. convenience
10. efficiency
11. argument
12. ridicule
13. marriage
14. conscientious
15. conceivable
16. tragedy
17. height
18. prevalent
19. benefited
20. referred
21. imaginary
22. psychology
23. therefore
24. environment
25. belief
26. maintenance
27. interpretation
28. experience
29. disappoint
30. precede
31. embarrass
32. beginning
33. disastrous
34. dissatisfied
35. hypocrite
36. criticize

ANSWERS TO FINAL TEST

Part I: Same Answers as Pre-Test

Part II:

1. admirable
2. alien
3. auxiliary
4. averse
5. bier
6. brief
7. Briton
8. cashier
9. ceiling
10. civilian
11. climactic
12. counterfeit
13. courageous
14. crotchet

15. deceitful
16. deign
17. deprecate
18. desirable
19. duly
20. either
21. elicit
22. exceed
23. excess
24. facetious
25. feign
26. fiend
27. fierce
28. fiery
29. gaiety
30. glacier
31. grief
32. likeable
33. medieval
34. mien
35. mischief
36. movable
37. neighbor
38. neither
39. outrageous
40. patient
41. peaceable
42. picnicking
43. pier
44. proficient
45. reprieve
46. seizure
47. sleigh
48. straight
49. trolleys
50. panicked